Hydrogeology and Steady-State Numerical Simulation of Groundwater Flow in the Lost Creek Designated Ground Water Basin, Weld, Adams, and Arapahoe Counties, Colorado

By L.R. Arnold

Prepared in cooperation with the Lost Creek Ground Water Management District and the Colorado Water Conservation Board

Scientific Investigations Report 2010–5082

U.S. Department of the Interior
U.S. Geological Survey

U.S. Department of the Interior
KEN SALAZAR, Secretary

U.S. Geological Survey
Marcia K. McNutt, Director

U.S. Geological Survey, Reston, Virginia: 2010

For more information on the USGS—the Federal source for science about the Earth, its natural and living resources, natural hazards, and the environment, visit http://www.usgs.gov or call 1-888-ASK-USGS

For an overview of USGS information products, including maps, imagery, and publications,
visit http://www.usgs.gov/pubprod

To order this and other USGS information products, visit http://store.usgs.gov

Suggested citation:
Arnold, L.R., 2010, Hydrogeology and steady-state numerical simulation of groundwater flow in the Lost Creek Designated Ground Water Basin, Weld, Adams, and Arapahoe Counties, Colorado: U.S. Geological Survey Scientific Investigations Report 2010–5082, 79 p.

Contents

Abstract 1

Introduction 2
  Purpose and Scope 2
  Study-Area Description 2
    Physiography and Climate 2
    Soils 4
    Land Use and Irrigation 4

Hydrogeology 8
  Aquifer Extent and Thickness 8
  Water Levels and Groundwater Flow 13
  Hydrologic Properties 13
  Recharge 18
    Precipitation Infiltration 18
    Stream-Channel Infiltration 25
    Deep Percolation of Water Applied to Irrigated Agricultural Fields 26
      Passive-Wick Lysimeters 26
      Water-Balance Method 29
    Ditch and Reservoir Seepage 30
    Subsurface Inflow 31
  Discharge 32
    Well Withdrawals 32
    Evapotranspiration 32
    Subsurface Outflow 32

Steady-State Numerical Simulation of Groundwater Flow 34
  Previous Groundwater Flow Model 34
    Design of Previous Model 34
    Inflows and Outflows Simulated by Previous Model 34
  Updated Groundwater Flow Model 34
    Design of Updated Model 35
    Boundary Conditions and Hydrologic Stresses 35
    Model Calibration 40
      Observations 40
      Prior Information 40
      Parameter Estimation 42
      Calibration Assessment 44
      Sensitivity Analysis 46
      Model Nonlinearity 46
    Simulation Results 47
    Model Limitations and Data Needs 49

Summary 51

Acknowledgments 52

References Cited 53

Appendix 1.   Gravimetric water content and chloride concentrations for soil samples collected
        in 2006 at six sites in the Lost Creek Designated Ground Water Basin, Colorado 59

Appendix 2.   Analytical quality-assurance and quality-control data for soil samples collected
        in 2006 at six sites in the Lost Creek Designated Ground Water Basin, Colorado 60

Appendix 3. Chloride in wet and dry deposition at the National Atmospheric Deposition
Program Pawnee site, Colorado 62
Appendix 4. Net irrigation, precipitation, and lysimeter-drainage data for sites in the Lost
Creek Designated Ground Water Basin, Colorado, 2007–2008 63
Appendix 5. Permitted acres, commingled acres, estimated irrigated acres, and estimated
average annual withdrawals from decreed irrigation wells with final permits in the
Lost Creek Designated Ground Water Basin, Colorado 74

Figures

1–9. Maps showing:
    1. Location of the Lost Creek Designated Ground Water Basin, in Weld, Adams,
        and Arapahoe Counties, Colorado 3
    2. Location of weather stations and the National Atmospheric Deposition Program
        site used by the study, Lost Creek Designated Ground Water Basin, Colorado 5
    3. Distribution of major soil associations in the Lost Creek Designated Ground
        Water Basin, Colorado 6
    4. Generalized land use in the Lost Creek Designated Ground Water
        Basin, Colorado..7
    5. Surficial geology of the Lost Creek Designated Ground Water Basin, Colorado 10
    6. Approximate thickness of regolith sediments in the Lost Creek Designated
        Ground Water Basin, Colorado 11
    7. Generalized altitude and configuration of the bedrock surface underlying
        regolith in the Lost Creek Designated Ground Water Basin, Colorado 12
    8. Ground-water levels at selected well locations in the Lost Creek Designated
        Ground Water Basin, Colorado 14
    9. Generalized configuration of the water table and extent of saturated
        sediments in the Lost Creek Designated Ground Water Basin, Colorado 15
   10. Plot showing relation of transmissivity determined from aquifer tests to transmissivity
        estimated from specific-capacity tests for 13 wells in the Lost Creek Designated
        Ground Water Basin 18
   11. Map showing hydraulic-conductivity distribution and location of aquifer tests
        and specific-capacity tests used to estimate hydraulic conductivity in the Lost Creek
        Designated Ground Water Basin, Colorado.. 19
   12. Map showing location of chloride-sampling sites and passive-wick lysimeters
        used for estimation of recharge beneath native grassland, nonirrigated agricultural
        fields, irrigated agricultural fields, and ephemeral stream channels in the Lost Creek
        Designated Ground Water Basin, Colorado.. 21
   13. Lithologic descriptions of soils at chloride-sampling sites used to estimate
        recharge beneath native grassland, nonirrigated agricultural fields, and ephemeral
        stream channels in the Lost Creek Designated Ground Water Basin, Colorado.............. 22
   14. Graph showing vertical profiles of chloride concentrations in soil water beneath
        native grassland, nonirrigated agricultural fields, and ephemeral stream channels
        in the Lost Creek Designated Ground Water Basin, Colorado 23
   15. Diagram of passive-wick lysimeter design and installation.. 27
16–21. Maps showing:
   16. Location of decreed irrigation wells with final permits in the Lost Creek
        Designated Ground Water Basin, Colorado.. 33
   17. Grid and boundary conditions of the groundwater flow model, Lost Creek
        Designated Ground Water Basin, Colorado.. 36
   18. Hydraulic conductivity zones of the groundwater flow model, Lost Creek
        Designated Ground Water Basin, Colorado.. 37

19. Recharge zones of the groundwater flow model, Lost Creek Designated Ground Water Basin, Colorado 38

20. Multiplier array used to increase recharge in areas representing sandy soils in the groundwater flow model, Lost Creek Designated Ground Water Basin, Colorado 39

21. Location of hydraulic-head observations used to calibrate the groundwater flow model, Lost Creek Designated Ground Water Basin, Colorado 41

22–25. Graphs showing:

22. Relation of weighted residuals to weighted simulated values in the groundwater flow model for (*A*) hydraulic head and prior information and (*B*) hydraulic head only, Lost Creek Designated Ground Water Basin, Colorado 45

23. Normal probability plot of weighted residuals for the groundwater flow model, Lost Creek Designated Ground Water Basin, Colorado 45

24. Relation of weighted observations to weighted simulated values in the groundwater flow model for (*A*) hydraulic head and prior information and (*B*) hydraulic head only, Lost Creek Designated Ground Water Basin, Colorado 46

25. Composite scaled sensitivities of parameters in the groundwater flow model, Lost Creek Designated Ground Water Basin, Colorado 47

26. Map showing steady-state altitude and configuration of the water table simulated by the groundwater flow model, Lost Creek Designated Ground Water Basin, Colorado 48

27. Map showing saturated thickness simulated by the groundwater flow model, Lost Creek Designated Ground Water Basin, Colorado 50

Tables

1. Annual water deliveries to irrigated agricultural fields in the Lost Creek Designated Ground Water Basin by Prospect Lateral Ditch, Lowline Canal, and the 1053 ditch, 1990–2001 9

2. Aquifer transmissivity and hydraulic conductivity determined from aquifer tests and estimated from specific capacity of wells in the Lost Creek Designated Ground Water Basin 16

3. Chloride concentration of soil water and precipitation, rate of precipitation, and recharge rates estimated from soil-chloride profiles beneath native grassland, nonirrigated agricultural fields, and ephemeral stream channels in the Lost Creek Designated Ground Water Basin 24

4. Net irrigation, precipitation, crop consumptive use, and recharge estimated by lysimeter drainage and a water-balance method for four irrigated agricultural fields in the Lost Creek Designated Ground Water Basin 28

5. Annual water deliveries to Olds Reservoir for recharge to the Lost Creek Designated Ground Water Basin 31

6. Hydraulic-head observations used to calibrate the Lost Creek Designated Ground Water Basin model 42

7. Initial and final parameter values, prior-information values, and prior-information weights used in the Lost Creek Designated Ground Water Basin model 43

8. Statistics used to assess calibration of the Lost Creek Designated Ground Water Basin model 44

9. Simulated steady-state groundwater budget of the Lost Creek Designated Ground Water Basin model representing conditions for 1990–2001 51

Conversion Factors

Inch/Pound to SI

Multiply	By	To obtain
Length		
inch (in.)	2.54	centimeter (cm)
foot (ft)	0.3048	meter (m)
mile (mi)	1.609	kilometer (km)
Area		
acre	4,047	square meter (m²)
square foot (ft²)	0.09290	square meter (m²)
square mile (mi²)	2.590	square kilometer (km²)
Volume		
gallon (gal)	3.785	liter (L)
cubic foot (ft³)	0.02832	cubic meter (m³)
acre-foot (acre-ft)	1,233	cubic meter (m³)
Flow rate		
acre-foot per day (acre-ft/d)	0.01427	cubic meter per second (m³/s)
acre-foot per year (acre-ft/yr)	1,233	cubic meter per year (m³/yr)
foot per day (ft/d)	0.3048	meter per day (m/d)
cubic foot per day (ft³/d)	0.02832	cubic meter per day (m³/d)
gallon per minute (gal/min)	0.06309	liter per second (L/s)
inch per hour (in/h)	0.0254	meter per hour (m/h)
inch per year (in/yr)	25.4	millimeter per year (mm/yr)
Specific capacity		
gallon per minute per foot [(gal/min)/ft)]	0.2070	liter per second per meter [(L/s)/m]
Hydraulic conductivity		
foot per day (ft/d)	0.3048	meter per day (m/d)
Hydraulic gradient		
foot per mile (ft/mi)	0.1894	meter per kilometer (m/km)
Transmissivity*		
foot squared per day (ft²/d)	0.09290	meter squared per day (m²/d)

Temperature in degrees Fahrenheit (°F) may be converted to degrees Celsius (°C) as follows:

$$°C=(°F-32)/1.8$$

Vertical coordinate information is referenced to the National Geodetic Vertical Datum of 1929 (NGVD 29).

Horizontal coordinate information is referenced to the North American Datum of 1983 (NAD 83).

Altitude, as used in this report, refers to distance above the vertical datum.

*Transmissivity: The standard unit for transmissivity is cubic foot per day per square foot times foot of aquifer thickness [(ft³/d)/ft²]ft. In this report, the mathematically reduced form, foot squared per day (ft²/d), is used for convenience.

SI to Inch/Pound

Multiply	By	To obtain
Length		
centimeter (cm)	0.3937	inch (in.)
meter (m)	3.281	foot (ft)
Volume		
cubic centimeter (cm³)	0.06102	cubic inch (in³)
liter (L)	61.02	cubic inch (in³)
Mass		
gram (g)	0.03527	ounce, avoirdupois (oz)
Pressure		
kilopascal (kPa)	0.1450	pound per square inch (lb/in²)

Concentrations of chemical constituents in water are given in milligrams per liter (mg/L).

Other abbreviations used in this report:

(MJ/m²)/d	Megajoule per square meter per day
kPa/°C	Kilopascal per degree Celsius
kg/m³	Kilogram per cubic meter
(MJ/kg)/°C	Megajoule per kilogram per degree Celsius
m/s	Meter per second
s/m	Second per meter
mm/d	Millimeters per day

Hydrogeology and Steady-State Numerical Simulation of Groundwater Flow in the Lost Creek Designated Ground Water Basin, Weld, Adams, and Arapahoe Counties, Colorado

By L.R. Arnold

Abstract

The Lost Creek Designated Ground Water Basin (Lost Creek basin) is an important alluvial aquifer for irrigation, public supply, and domestic water uses in northeastern Colorado. Urban growth in the adjacent Front Range urban corridor has increased demand for groundwater in the basin, and potential exportation of groundwater from the basin has raised concerns about the long-term sustainability and management of the basin's groundwater resources. Beginning in 2005, the U.S. Geological Survey, in cooperation with the Lost Creek Ground Water Management District and the Colorado Water Conservation Board, collected hydrologic data and constructed a numerical groundwater flow model of the Lost Creek basin. The steady-state model builds upon the work of previous investigators to provide an updated tool for simulating the potential effects of various hydrologic stresses on groundwater flow and evaluating possible aquifer-management strategies.

As part of model development, the thickness and extent of regolith sediments in the basin were mapped, and data were collected concerning aquifer recharge beneath native grassland, nonirrigated agricultural fields, irrigated agricultural fields, and ephemeral stream channels. The thickness and extent of regolith in the Lost Creek basin indicate the presence of a 2- to 7-mile-wide buried paleovalley that extends along the Lost Creek basin from south to north, where it joins the alluvial valley of the South Platte River valley. Regolith that fills the paleovalley is as much as about 190 ft thick. Recharge from infiltration of precipitation on native grassland and nonirrigated agricultural fields was estimated by using the chloride mass-balance method at four sites in the Lost Creek basin. Recharge from infiltration of ephemeral streamflow was estimated by using apparent downward velocities of chloride peaks in soil profiles at two sites in the basin. Recharge from deep percolation of water applied to irrigated agricultural fields was estimated by using passive-wick lysimeters installed at four sites in the basin and by using a water-balance approach. Average annual recharge from infiltration of precipitation on native grassland and nonirrigated agricultural fields was estimated to range from 0.1 to 0.6 inch, which represents about 1–4 percent of long-term average precipitation. Average annual recharge from infiltration of ephemeral streamflow was estimated to range from 5.7 to 8.2 inches. Average annual recharge beneath irrigated agricultural fields was estimated to range from 0 to 11.3 inches, depending on irrigation method, soil type, crop type, and the net quantity of irrigation water applied. Estimated average annual recharge beneath irrigated agricultural fields represents about 0–43 percent of net irrigation.

The U.S. Geological Survey modular groundwater modeling program, MODFLOW–2000, was used to develop a steady-state groundwater flow model of the Lost Creek basin. The model primarily was calibrated to average hydrologic conditions representing the period 1990–2001 by using the inverse modeling capabilities of MODFLOW–2000. Simulated water levels generally have acceptable agreement with water levels measured at 43 locations in the Lost Creek basin, and calibration statistics indicate that residuals between simulated and measured values of hydraulic head likely are random, independent, and normally distributed. Composite scaled sensitivities were highest for parameters representing withdrawals from wells lacking pumping data, recharge beneath nonirrigated areas, and recharge beneath flood-irrigated fields, indicating that these parameters likely are the most important to accurately define for model simulations.

Groundwater in the simulated Lost Creek basin generally flows from basin margins toward the center of the basin and northward along the paleovalley of the basin. The largest source of inflow to the model occurs from recharge beneath flood- and sprinkler-irrigated agricultural fields (14,510 acre-ft/yr), which represents 39.7 percent of total simulated inflow. Other substantial sources of inflow to the model are recharge from precipitation and stream-channel infiltration in nonirrigated areas (13,810 acre-feet per year [acre-ft/yr]), seepage from Olds Reservoir (4,280 acre-ft/yr), and subsurface inflow from ditches and irrigated fields outside the model domain (2,490 acre-ft/yr), which contribute 37.7, 11.7, and 6.8 percent, respectively, of total inflow. The largest outflow from the model occurs from irrigation well withdrawals (26,760 acre-ft/yr), which represent 73.2 percent of total outflow. Groundwater discharge (6,640 acre-ft/yr) at the downgradient end of the Lost Creek basin represents 18.2 percent of total outflow, and evapotranspiration (3,140 acre-ft/yr) represents about 8.6 percent of total outflow.

Introduction

The Lost Creek Designated Ground Water Basin (Lost Creek basin; fig. 1) consists of an alluvial aquifer that is an important source of water for irrigation, public supply, and domestic use in northeastern Colorado. Perennial streams do not exist within the basin, and groundwater in the basin historically has been used primarily for irrigation of agricultural land within the basin's boundaries. However, urban growth in the adjacent Front Range urban corridor has increased demand for groundwater in the basin, and potential exportation of groundwater from the basin has raised concerns about the long-term sustainability and management of the basin's groundwater resources.

The hydrogeology and groundwater resources of the Lost Creek basin originally were characterized in 1967 by Nelson, Haley, Patterson,and Quirk, Inc. (1967) in a report to the Colorado Ground Water Commission. The purpose of the report was to provide information for legally defining the basin as a Designated Ground Water Basin, subject to a set of water rules separate from the Doctrine of Prior Appropriation used for regulation of tributary waters in the State of Colorado. Designated groundwater in alluvial aquifers generally is defined as groundwater in areas not adjacent to a continuously flowing natural stream wherein groundwater withdrawals have constituted the principal water usage for at least 15 years (Jones and Cech, 2009). Data from the Nelson, Haley, Patterson, and Quirk, Inc. report were used in the development of a steady-state numerical groundwater flow model of the Lost Creek basin in 1995 (Thomas Hatton, J.R. Engineering, Inc., written commun., 2004), and the model subsequently was modified between 1995 and 2004 (Barbara Ford, HRS Water Consultants, Inc., written commun., 2005) for use in simulating the effects of several pumping scenarios under different recharge and hydrogeologic conditions. Since development of the previous groundwater models, new hydrogeologic information has been collected in the Lost Creek basin as part of the U.S. Geological Survey (USGS) National Water Quality Assessment (NAWQA) program and the State of Colorado's South Platte Decision Support System (SPDSS) program.

In 2005 the USGS began a study in cooperation with the Lost Creek Ground Water Management District to review and summarize the 2004 version of the existing groundwater model and to construct an updated numerical groundwater flow model of the Lost Creek basin using new data and numerical simulation capabilities. In 2007, the study was expanded in cooperation with the Colorado Water Conservation Board to collect data concerning aquifer recharge occurring from deep percolation of water applied to agricultural fields within the basin in order to improve estimates of irrigation recharge and reduce model uncertainty as related to irrigation recharge.

Purpose and Scope

The purpose of this report is to describe the hydrogeology and a steady-state numerical groundwater flow model of the Lost Creek Designated Ground Water Basin in Weld, Adams, and Arapahoe Counties in Colorado. The description of hydrogeology provides new information, with particular emphasis on aquifer geometry and recharge, that builds upon the work of previous investigators. The steady-state model also builds upon the work of previous investigators to provide an updated tool for simulating the potential effects of various hydrologic stresses on groundwater flow and evaluating possible aquifer-management strategies.

The extent and thickness of regolith (unconsolidated sediments) in the basin were mapped to better characterize the subsurface geometry of the basin. Water-level data were compiled for the period 1990–2001 for use in calibrating the steady-state groundwater flow model. Data concerning infiltration of precipitation, infiltration from stream channels, deep percolation of water applied to irrigated agricultural fields, ditch and reservoir seepage, and subsurface inflow were collected to improve estimates of recharge to the basin. Data concerning well withdrawals, evapotranspiration, and subsurface outflow were used to estimate discharge from the basin. The USGS modular groundwater modeling program MODFLOW–2000 (Harbaugh and others, 2000; Hill and others, 2000) was used to construct and calibrate the updated steady-state groundwater flow model using inverse-modeling methods.

Study-Area Description

The Lost Creek basin occupies an area of about 432 square miles (mi^2) in parts of Weld, Adams, and Arapahoe Counties in northeastern Colorado (fig. 1). The administrative boundary of the Lost Creek basin is defined approximately by the drainage basin of Lost Creek and its tributaries. Population centers in the basin include the towns of Keenesburg, Roggen, Prospect Valley, and Bennett. The Lost Creek basin is about 43 mi long and extends from about 6 mi south of Bennett northward to the South Platte River valley. The basin is as much as 14 mi wide.

Physiography and Climate

The Lost Creek basin lies within the Colorado Piedmont section of the Great Plains physiographic province (Fenneman, 1946) and generally is characterized by relatively flat to gently sloping terrain with local relief of tens of feet. North of Roggen,

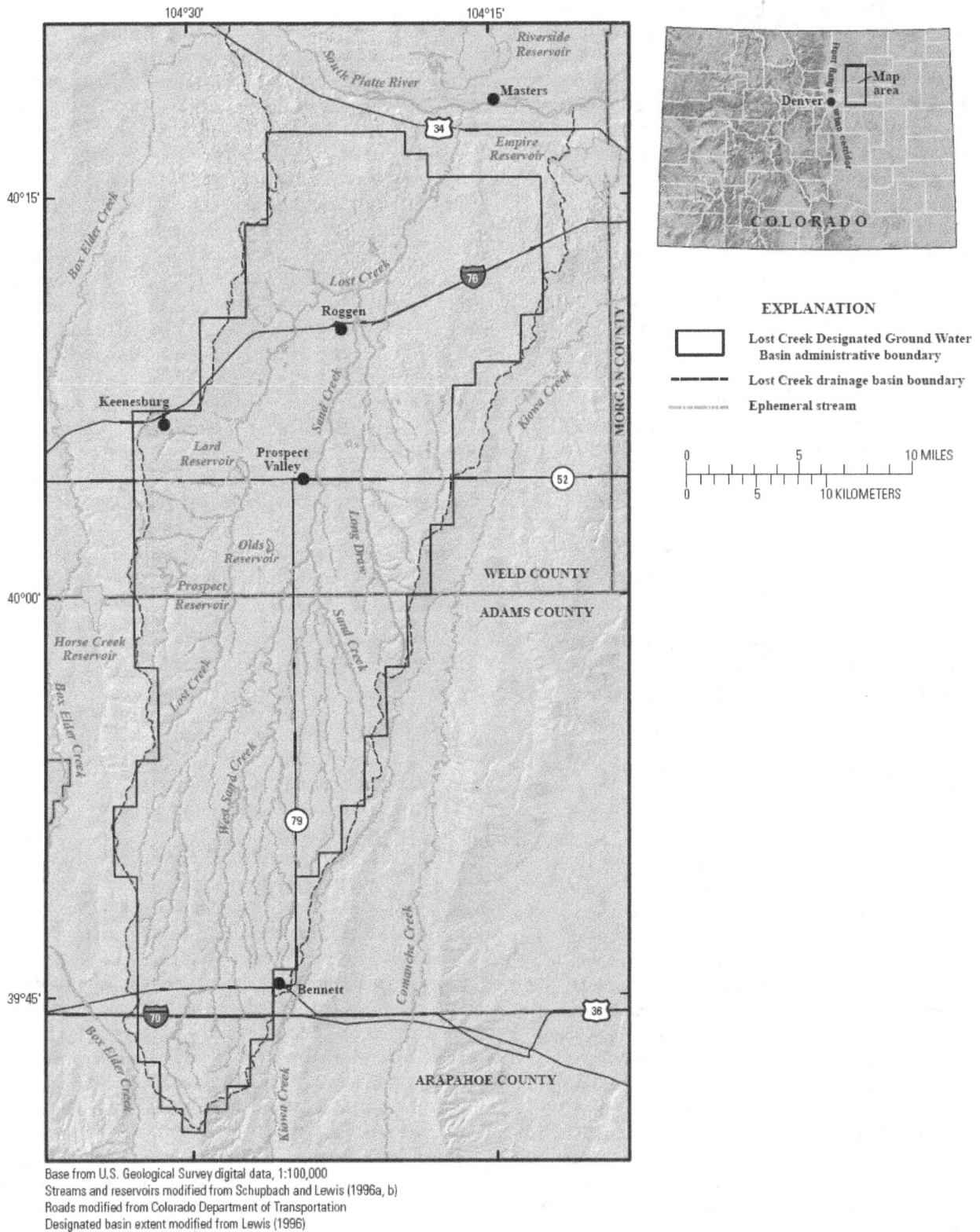

104°30'   104°15'

40°15'

40°00'

39°45'

Figure 1.   Location of the Lost Creek Designated Ground Water Basin, in Weld, Adams, and Arapahoe Counties, Colorado.

the landscape is composed largely of vegetated sand dunes, and topography commonly is hilly. Land-surface altitudes in the Lost Creek basin range from about 4,550 ft, where the Lost Creek channel exits the north end of the basin, to about 5,880 ft at the southern end of the basin. Three reservoirs (Prospect, Lord, and Olds) are located in the Lost Creek basin (fig. 1). Prospect and Lord Reservoirs are used primarily for storage and delivery of irrigation water to agricultural fields in the Lost Creek basin. Olds Reservoir is used primarily to recharge groundwater in the Lost Creek basin through lakebed seepage. No perennial streams exist in the Lost Creek basin, but drainage in ephemeral streams generally is northward toward the South Platte River. Primary ephemeral stream channels in the Lost Creek basin are Lost Creek, Sand Creek, West Sand Creek, and Long Draw, which usually are dry except after significant storm events. Based on discussions with local residents of the Lost Creek basin, Skinner (1963) reported that, historically, Lost Creek had stormflow about once every 2 years on average, and Sand Creek had stormflow an average of about twice per year. Long Draw historically has had stormflow about once every 2 years (John Cordes, Lost Creek Ground Water Management District, oral commun., 2006). Since 2000, streams generally have had stormflow an average of about once every 3 years (Thomas Sauter and Kent Crisman, Lost Creek Ground Water Management District, oral commun., 2008). When streams do flow after storms, runoff seeps rapidly into the ground. Any runoff in upper Lost Creek is captured by Lord Reservoir (Code, 1945; Skinner, 1963), and runoff in Sand Creek and Long Draw rarely reaches the town of Roggen (John Cordes, Lost Creek Ground Water Management District, oral commun., 2006). Runoff from rainstorms typically lasts less than 1 day, and runoff from local snowmelt typically lasts less than 1 week (Skinner, 1963).

The Lost Creek basin has a semiarid continental climate with large differences in temperature between summer and winter; sudden and extreme temperature changes on a daily basis are common. Temperatures recorded at three long-term weather stations (Brighton, period of record 1973–2007; Byers 5 ENE, period of record 1893–2007; Fort Morgan, period of record 1896–2008) (fig. 2) near the Lost Creek basin range from a mean monthly low of 9.6°F during January to a mean monthly high of 90.3°F during July (Western Regional Climate Center, 2008). Long-term average annual precipitation for the periods of record at the three weather stations ranged from 13.3 to 14.8 inches (Western Regional Climate Center, 2008) with a mean value of 14.1 inches. Average annual pan evaporation measured at the Wiggins 7 SW weather station (period of record 1960–1971) (fig. 2) near the Lost Creek basin was 54.1 inches (Western Regional Climate Center, 2008), which greatly exceeds average annual precipitation in the basin. About 70–80 percent of annual precipitation and about 88 percent of annual evapotranspiration in the Lost Creek basin occurs from April through September.

Soils

Soils in the Lost Creek basin consist of six general soil associations—Weld-Norka-Adena, Valent-Julesburg-Vona, Otero-Thedalund-Olney, Altvan-Dacono-Nunn, Heldt-Nunn-Limon, and Kutch-Bresser-Louviers (U.S. Department of Agriculture, 1994) (fig. 3). Most soils south of Roggen are composed of loam or silt loam of the Weld-Norka-Adena group with soil permeability generally ranging from 0.2 to 2 in/hr (Heil and others, 1978). Sand dunes north of Roggen are composed almost entirely of the Valent-Julesburg-Vona group with soil permeability generally ranging from 2 to 20 in/hr. Soils of the Altvan-Dacono-Nunn group are located along the stream channels of Lost Creek, Sand Creek, and West Sand Creek (fig. 3), and soils of the Otero-Thedalund-Olney group cover localized areas in the central and southern parts of the basin. Soils of the Altvan-Dacono-Nunn group generally are composed of clay loam to sandy loam and have permeability (0.2–2 in/hr) similar to soils of the Weld-Norka-Adena group (Heil and others, 1978). Soils of the Otero-Thedalund-Olney group are composed of loam to loam sand and have permeability (0.6–20 in/hr) similar to soils of the Valent-Julesburg-Vona group. Soils of the Heldt-Nunn-Limon and Kutch-Bresser-Louviers groups cover small areas at the southern end of the basin.

Land Use and Irrigation

Land in the Lost Creek basin is used primarily for agriculture and rangeland (fig. 4), but small areas of urban and other land uses also occur in the basin. Irrigated agricultural land primarily is located in the central and northern parts of the basin, and nonirrigated agricultural land primarily is in the southern part of the basin and near the basin margins. Rangeland is prominent in the northern part of the basin where soils are highly permeable and hilly topography exists. Based on mapping of irrigated acres (Riverside Technology, Inc., 2007) (fig. 4), about 32,500 acres in the Lost Creek basin were irrigated in 2001. About 57 percent of the area was irrigated using flood-irrigation methods and about 43 percent was irrigated by sprinklers. Crops commonly grown in the irrigated parts of the basin include corn, wheat, barley, alfalfa, and small vegetables (Richard Huwa, Lost Creek Ground Water Management District, oral commun., 2007). Dryland crops cultivated in the nonirrigated parts of the basin consist mainly of wheat and other small grains.

Both surface water and groundwater are used for irrigation in the Lost Creek basin, and a parcel of irrigated agricultural land may be supported by surface water, groundwater, or both. Surface water is conveyed to the Lost Creek basin by the Denver-Hudson Canal (fig. 4) and is stored in Prospect and Lord Reservoirs. Surface water is delivered to agricultural

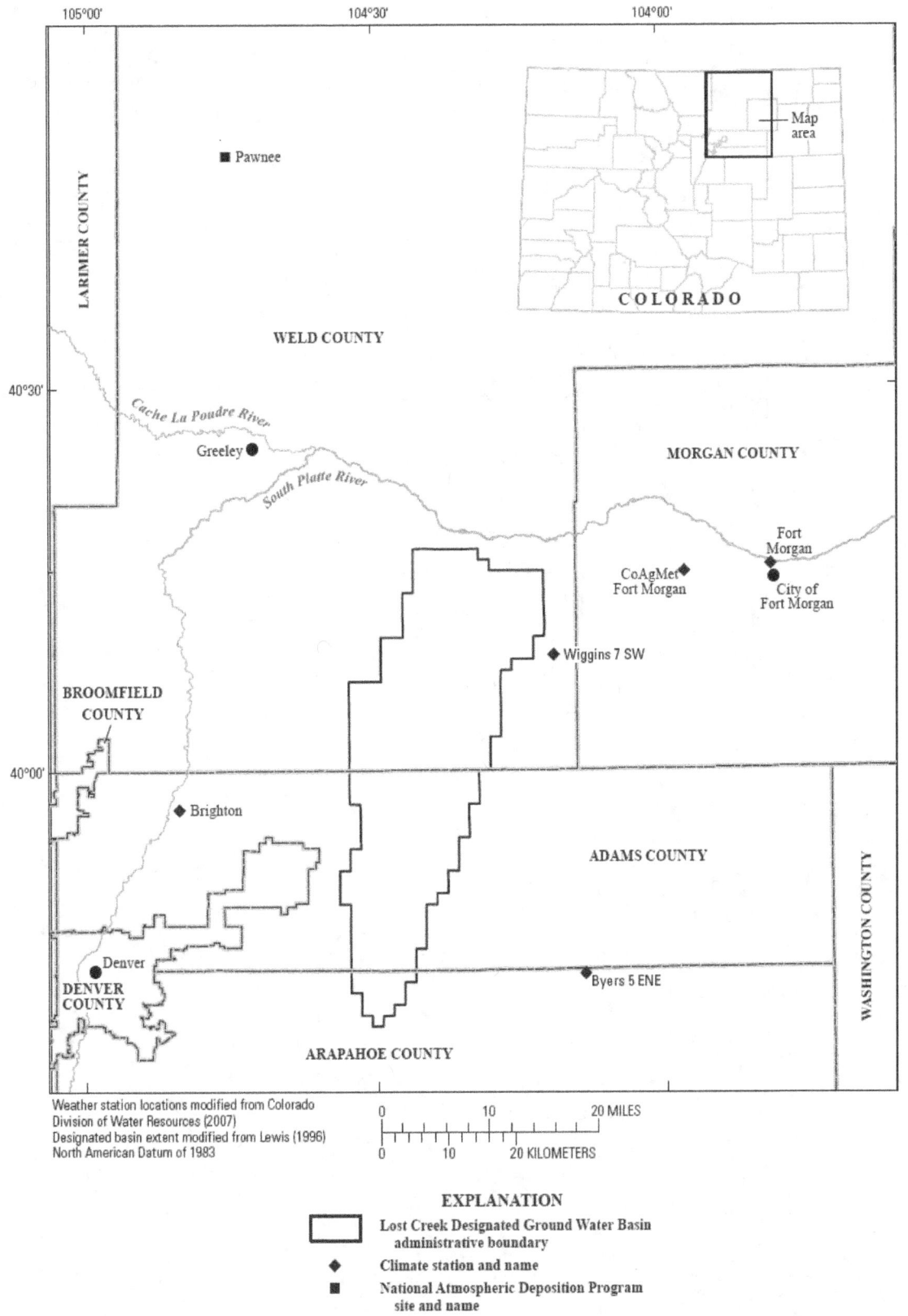

Figure 2. Location of weather stations and the National Atmospheric Deposition Program site used by the study, Lost Creek Designated Ground Water Basin, Colorado.

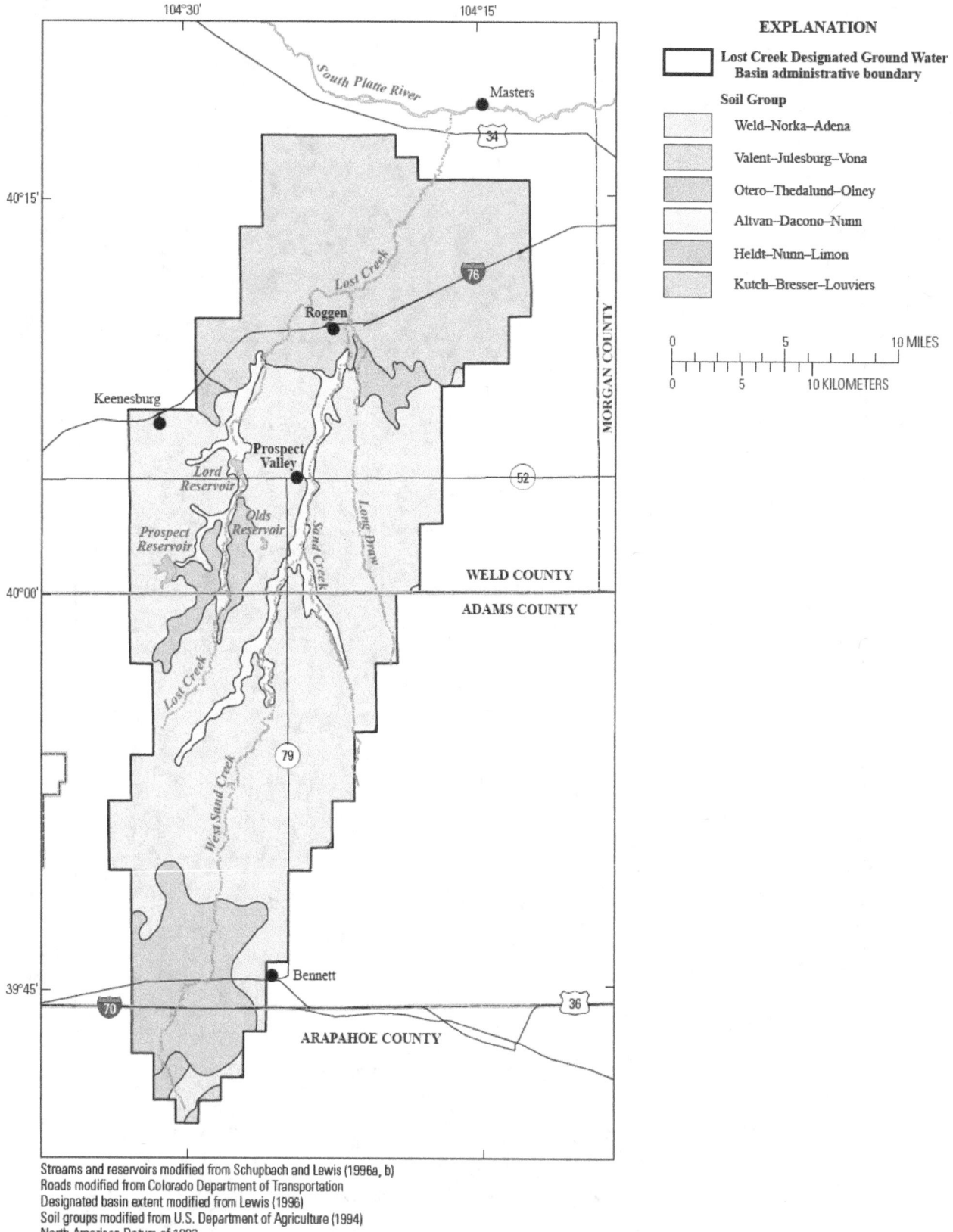

Streams and reservoirs modified from Schupbach and Lewis (1996a, b)
Roads modified from Colorado Department of Transportation
Designated basin extent modified from Lewis (1996)
Soil groups modified from U.S. Department of Agriculture (1994)
North American Datum of 1983

Figure 3.   Distribution of major soil associations in the Lost Creek Designated Ground Water Basin, Colorado.

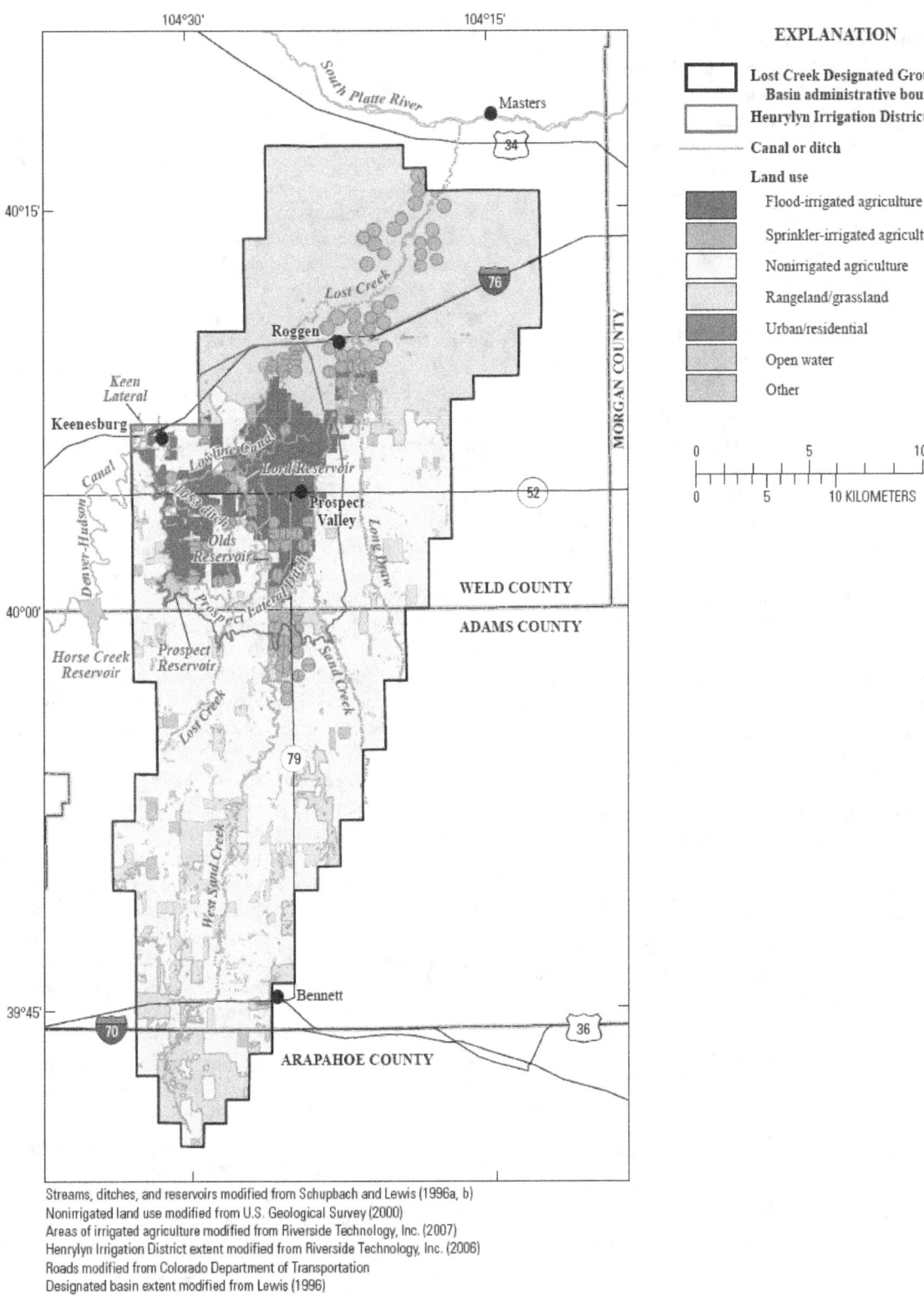

Streams, ditches, and reservoirs modified from Schupbach and Lewis (1996a, b)
Nonirrigated land use modified from U.S. Geological Survey (2000)
Areas of irrigated agriculture modified from Riverside Technology, Inc. (2007)
Henrylyn Irrigation District extent modified from Riverside Technology, Inc. (2006)
Roads modified from Colorado Department of Transportation
Designated basin extent modified from Lewis (1996)
North American Datum of 1983

Figure 4. Generalized land use in the Lost Creek Designated Ground Water Basin, Colorado.

fields in the basin by the Henrylyn Irrigation District (fig. 4) primarily by using Prospect Lateral Ditch, Lowline Canal, and the 1053 ditch (Rodney Baumgartner, Henrylyn Irrigation District, oral commun., 2008). Prospect Lateral Ditch is used to deliver releases from Prospect Reservoir to irrigated fields in the Lost Creek basin. Lowline Canal and the 1053 ditch divert water directly from the Denver-Hudson Canal before it reaches Prospect Reservoir. Lowline Canal also is used to deliver releases from Lord Reservoir to irrigated fields. Surface water also is delivered to agricultural fields in the Lost Creek basin by using Keen Lateral, but the number of acres (about 200–300) estimated by this study to be irrigated by Keen Lateral within the boundaries of the basin represents only a small portion of the total irrigated land area in the basin.

An average of about 4,300 acre-ft of water was delivered annually by Prospect Lateral Ditch during the period 1990–2001 (Rodney Baumgartner, Henrylyn Irrigation District, written commun., 2008) (table 1) to irrigate about 9,600 acres, which amounts to about 0.45 acre-ft of water per acre of land, not considering seepage or other conveyance losses. During the same time period, average annual deliveries by Lowline Canal were about 2,800 acre-ft of water to irrigate about 6,500 acres, amounting to about 0.43 acre-ft of water per acre of land, and average annual deliveries by the 1053 ditch were about 4,700 acre-ft for irrigation of about 6,000 acres, amounting to about 0.78 acre-ft of water per acre of land. In all, an average of about 11,900 acre-ft of surface water was used to irrigate about 22,100 acres in the Lost Creek basin, amounting to about 0.54 acre-ft of water per acre of land.

About 266 decreed irrigation wells with final permits are located in the Lost Creek basin (Suzanne Sellers, Colorado Division of Water Resources, written commun., 2007). Assuming each of these wells was actively used during 1990–2001, it is estimated by this study that an average of about 44,300 acre-ft of groundwater was withdrawn annually to irrigate about 27,800 acres in the Lost Creek basin, providing about 1.6 acre-ft of water per acre of land. Groundwater withdrawals for irrigation are discussed in more detail in the "Well Withdrawals" section of this report.

The discrepancy between the sum of acres irrigated by surface water and groundwater (49,900) and the total number of irrigated acres (32,500) mapped by Riverside Technology, Inc. (2007) may reflect that some parcels are irrigated by both surface water and groundwater. Alternatively, the discrepancy may indicate inaccuracies in the estimates of irrigated acres, particularly the estimate of acres irrigated by groundwater, which is based on the number of acres permitted for each well. If not all wells actively withdrew water during 1990–2001, the number of acres irrigated by groundwater and total annual groundwater withdrawals might be overestimated. Based on a total irrigated land area of 32,500 acres, total irrigation by both surface water and groundwater (56,200 acre-ft) represents an average application of about 1.73 acre-ft of water per acre of land.

Hydrogeology

Aquifer Extent and Thickness

The Lost Creek basin alluvial aquifer occupies a paleovalley (ancient buried stream valley) adjoining the South Platte River valley. The sides and southern end of the alluvial aquifer are defined by uplands composed of bedrock that crops out or forms shallow subcrops near the land surface. The northern end of the Lost Creek basin connects to the alluvial aquifer of the South Platte River valley. Alluvial sediments in the Lost Creek basin locally are covered by eolian (windblown) sand deposits, particularly in the northern part of the basin (Braddock and Cole, 1978; Bryant and others, 1981) (fig. 5). Bedrock underlying the Lost Creek basin consists of sedimentary strata that constitute the Denver Basin aquifer system (Robson, 1987). The southern part of the alluvial aquifer is directly underlain by the Denver aquifer, the central part of the aquifer is directly underlain by the Arapahoe aquifer, and the northern part of the aquifer is directly underlain by the Laramie–Fox Hills aquifer.

To determine the subsurface configuration of the Lost Creek basin for input to the updated groundwater model, the thickness of regolith sediments (primarily alluvium and eolian deposits) in the basin was mapped using data compiled from Bjorklund and Brown (1957), Nelson, Haley, Patterson, and Quirk, Inc. (1967), Skinner (1963), Hurr and others (1972), HRS Water Consultants, Inc. (written commun., 2006), and about 550 lithologic logs from wells and test holes on file with the USGS Colorado Water Science Center in Lakewood, Colorado and the Colorado Division of Water Resources (CDWR) in Denver, Colorado. In some places, weathered bedrock may have been mapped as regolith because of inaccurate lithologic logs or an indistinct contact between regolith and the underlying bedrock. In particular, lithologic logs of deep wells completed in bedrock were used to map regolith thickness in the southern part of the basin where few other data were available, and regolith thickness determined from these logs might not be accurate because they commonly lacked detailed regolith information.

Regolith-thickness contours were prepared by hand contouring regolith-thickness data. Hand contouring, rather than automated methods, was used to better interpret the varied and inconsistent data values that sometimes resulted from local irregularities in the bedrock surface, the imprecise bedrock contact, mislocated data points, or conflicting data. Regolith-thickness contours generally were drawn using the preponderance of data in a local area and do not necessarily agree with each individual data value. Regolith-thickness data were contoured using a 20-ft contour interval with consideration of apparent data quality, topography, lithology, surface geology, and understanding of likely depositional and erosional processes leading to the formation of the Lost Creek alluvial valley. In areas where regolith-thickness data were unavailable, the base of the Lost Creek basin determined by Nelson, Haley, Patterson, and Quirk (1967, pl. 2) was used to estimate regolith thickness. Mapping results (figs. 6 and 7) indicate a well-defined paleovalley that extends along the Lost

Table 1. Annual water deliveries to irrigated agricultural fields in the Lost Creek Designated Ground Water Basin by Prospect Lateral Ditch, Lowline Canal, and the 1053 ditch, 1990–2001.

[--, no data]

Year	Prospect Lateral Ditch			Lowline Canal			1053 ditch			Total		
	Total water delivered[1] (acre-feet)	Irrigated area[2] (acres)	Effective water application[3] (acre-foot/acre)	Total water delivered[1] (acre-feet)	Irrigated area[2] (acres)	Effective water application[3] (acre-foot/acre)	Total water delivered[1] (acre-feet)	Irrigated area[2] (acres)	Effective water application[3] (acre-foot/acre)	Total water delivered[1] (acre-feet)	Irrigated area[2] (acres)	Effective water application[3] (acre-foot/acre)
1990	1,947	9,632	0.20	2,480	6,453	0.38	4,005	6,004	0.67	8,432	22,089	0.38
1991	3,897	9,632	0.40	2,834	6,453	0.44	4,936	6,004	0.82	11,667	22,089	0.53
1992	3,605	9,632	0.37	2,471	6,453	0.38	3,906	6,004	0.65	9,982	22,089	0.45
1993	3,785	9,632	0.39	2,517	6,453	0.39	4,015	6,004	0.67	10,317	22,089	0.47
1994	3,695	9,632	0.38	2,457	6,453	0.38	4,516	6,004	0.75	10,668	22,089	0.48
1995	4,734	9,632	0.49	2,819	6,453	0.44	5,200	6,004	0.87	12,753	22,089	0.58
1996	3,918	9,632	0.41	2,903	6,453	0.45	4,775	6,004	0.80	11,596	22,089	0.52
1997	5,515	9,632	0.57	3,278	6,453	0.51	5,902	6,004	0.98	14,695	22,089	0.67
1998	6,979	9,632	0.72	3,630	6,453	0.56	6,187	6,004	1.03	16,796	22,089	0.76
1999	6,611	9,632	0.69	3,238	6,453	0.50	4,826	6,004	0.80	14,675	22,089	0.66
2000	3,511	9,632	0.36	2,193	6,453	0.34	3,335	6,004	0.56	9,039	22,089	0.41
2001	3,573	9,632	0.37	--	6,453	--	--	6,004	--	--	22,089	--
Average	4,314	9,632	0.45	2,802	6,453	0.43	4,691	6,004	0.78	11,875	22,089	0.54

[1]Total water delivered provided by Rodney Baumgartner, Henrylyn Irrigation District, written commun., 2008.

[2]Irrigated area based on 1990 acreage provided by Rodney Baumgartner, Henrylyn Irrigation District, written commun., 2008.

[3]Effective water applications assumes no conveyance loss.

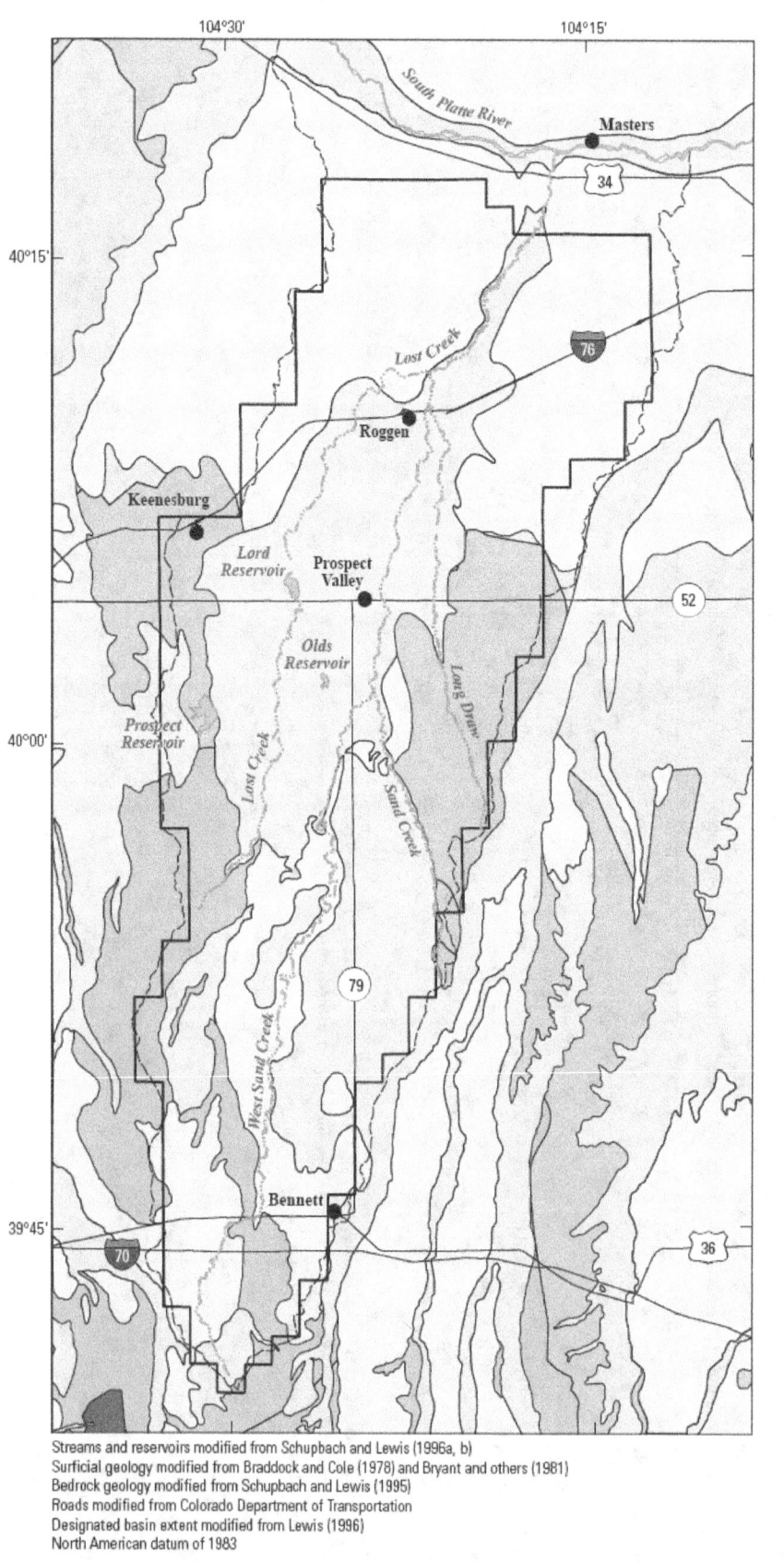

EXPLANATION

Lost Creek Designated Ground Water Basin administrative boundary

Lost Creek drainage basin boundary

Hydrogeologic unit

Eolian deposits (Quaternary)

Alluvium (Quaternary)

Upper Dawson aquifer (Tertiary)

Denver aquifer (Tertiary/Cretaceous)

Arapahoe aquifer (Cretaceous)

Laramie Formation (Cretaceous)

Laramie–Fox Hills aquifer (Cretaceous)

Streams and reservoirs modified from Schupbach and Lewis (1996a, b)
Surficial geology modified from Braddock and Cole (1978) and Bryant and others (1981)
Bedrock geology modified from Schupbach and Lewis (1995)
Roads modified from Colorado Department of Transportation
Designated basin extent modified from Lewis (1996)
North American datum of 1983

Figure 5.   Surficial geology of the Lost Creek Designated Ground Water Basin, Colorado.

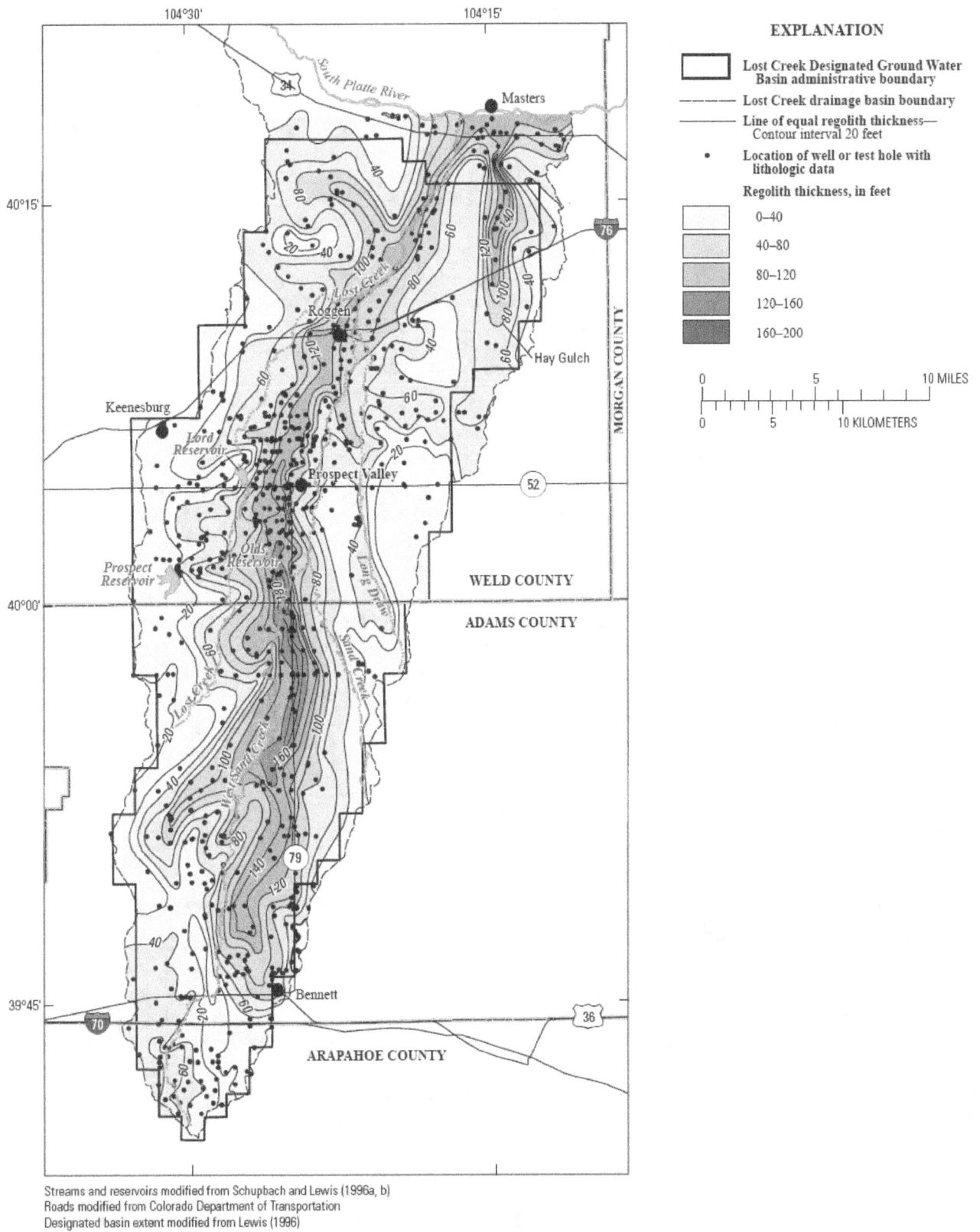

Figure 6. Approximate thickness of regolith sediments in the Lost Creek Designated Ground Water Basin, Colorado.

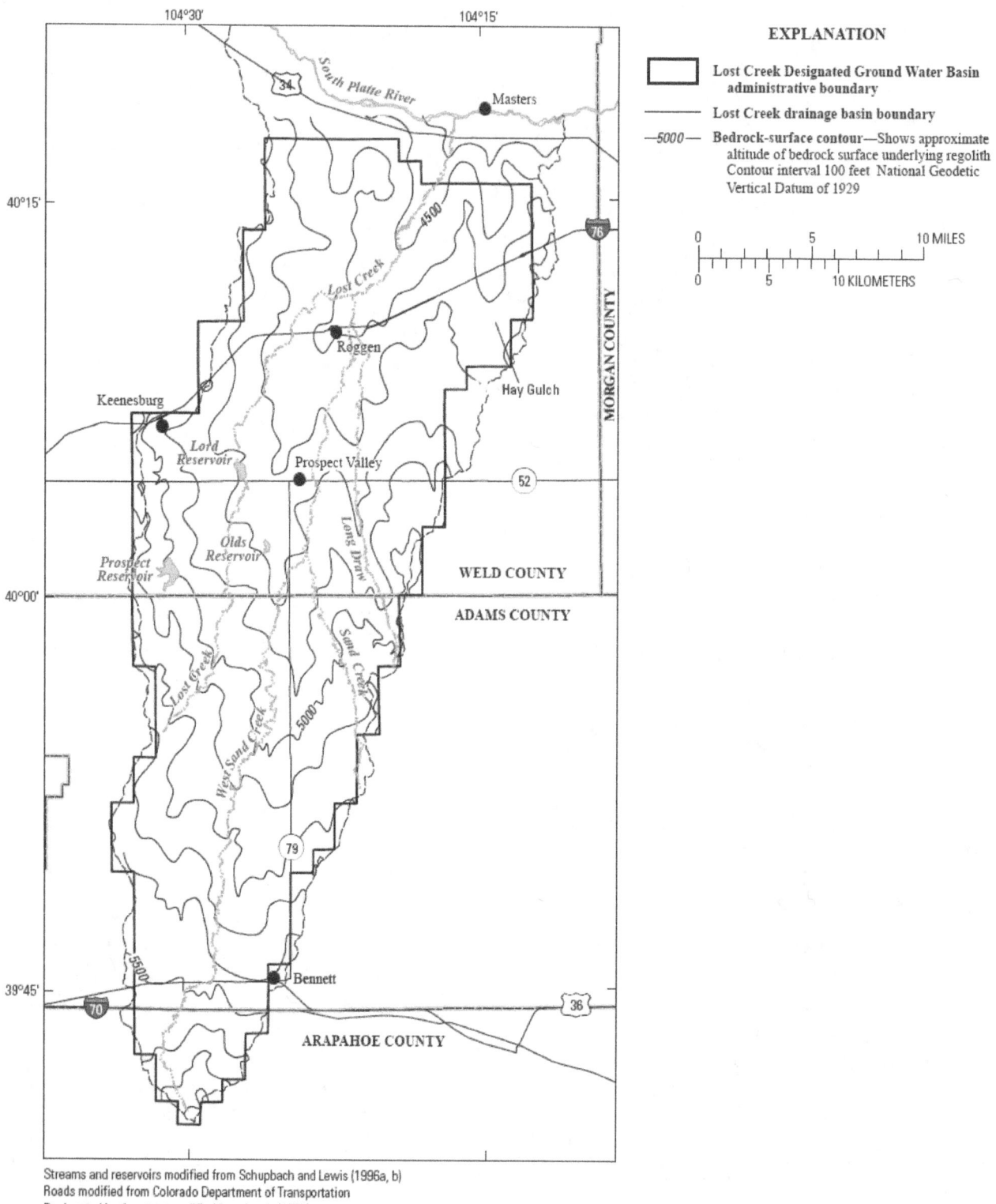

Figure 7.   Generalized altitude and configuration of the bedrock surface underlying regolith in the Lost Creek Designated Ground Water Basin, Colorado.

Creek basin from south to north, where it joins the alluvial valley of the South Platte River. Regolith along the main part of the paleovalley is as much as about 190 ft thick, and several smaller paleovalleys (such as along Long Draw and west of West Sand Creek in the southern part of the basin) appear tributary to the main paleovalley and have regolith as much as 120 ft thick. In the area of Hay Gulch, a substantial paleovalley appears to be separated from the main paleovalley of the Lost Creek basin by a ridge of relatively shallow bedrock. However, few data were available to map regolith thickness in the area between Hay Gulch and the main paleovalley. The extent of the main paleovalley and Hay Gulch generally coincides with the extent of alluvial and eolian sediments mapped by Braddock and Cole (1978) and Bryant and others (1981). However, some areas mapped as bedrock at the land surface by the two investigations were found to have regolith sediments generally 20–40 ft thick based on borehole information, particularly in the area of upper Long Draw. Discrepancies between the maps of surficial geology and regolith thickness might be the result of poorly exposed outcrops, relatively soft weathered bedrock at the land surface being mapped as regolith, or the different scales at which the maps were prepared. Geographic Information System datasets (Arnold, 2010) showing regolith-thickness and bedrock-altitude data, regolith-thickness contours, and raster-based regolith thickness are available at *http://water.usgs.gov/lookup/getgislist*.

Examination of lithologic logs along and in cross section to the main paleovalley and its tributaries indicates sediments along the deepest part of the paleovalleys are composed primarily of sand and gravel with interbedded clay layers. Sediments adjacent to the deepest part of paleovalleys generally appear to have approximately equal amounts of sand, gravel, and clay, and clay content generally increases toward paleovalley margins except where thick eolian (windblown) sands are present at the land surface. In topographically high areas at the edges of paleovalleys, bedrock commonly is at or near land surface and sediments generally are composed primarily of clay.

Water Levels and Groundwater Flow

Groundwater levels in the study area (fig. 8) generally are highest in winter and early spring before the irrigation season and generally decline during the summer season as a result of pumping for irrigation. The magnitude of groundwater-level fluctuations between seasons and from year to year varies by location. Long-term historical water levels measured in the Lost Creek basin (Colorado Division of Water Resources, 2000; Schaubs, 2007) indicate seasonal and yearly groundwater-level fluctuations generally range from about 0 to 3 ft throughout most of the basin. Groundwater-level fluctuations are greater (generally 1–5 ft) in and immediately downgradient from irrigated areas in the Henrylyn Irrigation District (well GS–2), and they are greatest (generally 2–10 ft) downgradient from Olds Reservoir (well GS–3). Groundwater levels in and immediately downgradient from irrigated areas in the Henrylyn Irrigation District commonly rose about 10–25 ft during the early to mid-1980s,

remained relatively stable from 1990 through the spring of 2002, and began declining in 2003. Groundwater levels in the Lost Creek basin north of Roggen (well N–8) generally have declined a total of 3 to 10 ft in a relatively steady manner since the early 1980s. Well GS–6 is the only site for which long-term water-level measurements were available upgradient from the area irrigated by the Henrylyn Irrigation District. Groundwater levels at well GS–6 rose about 8 ft gradually during the 1980s and declined about 5 ft gradually from the mid-1990s through 2006. Groundwater-level fluctuations in the Lost Creek basin likely are caused by differences in recharge from infiltration of precipitation and ephemeral stream water, deep percolation of water applied to irrigated agricultural fields, seepage beneath reservoirs and irrigation ditches, and groundwater withdrawals from wells.

Groundwater in the Lost Creek basin flows generally northward under unconfined conditions toward the South Platte River valley with hydraulic gradients ranging from about 10 to 80 ft/mi (Nelson, Haley, Patterson, and Quirk, Inc., 1967, pl. 3) (fig. 9). The steeper gradients generally occur in the southern part of the basin and along basin margins. Saturated thickness in the Lost Creek basin ranges from zero near the basin margins to about 120 ft in the north-central part of the basin (Nelson, Haley, Patterson, and Quirk, Inc., 1967, pl. 3). The water table in the northern part of the Lost Creek basin generally is 10 to 50 ft below land surface but can be less than 10 ft below land surface in some topographically low areas. The water table in the southern part of the Lost Creek basin generally is about 50 to 130 ft below land surface.

Hydrologic Properties

Aquifer transmissivity of the Lost Creek basin was estimated for this study from the results of 14 aquifer tests presented in published reports (Bjorklund and Brown, 1957; Skinner, 1963; Nelson, Haley, Patterson, and Quirk, Inc., 1967; Wilson, 1965) and consultant reports (JR Engineering, written commun., 2005; HRS Water Consultants, Inc., written commun., 2006) and from specific-capacity data from well-construction records on file with USGS and CDWR (table 2). The method of Theis and others (1963, p. 331–341) was used to estimate aquifer transmissivity from specific-capacity data by using a modified form of Theis's equation 1 as presented by Prudic (1991). The modified form of the equation is given as:

$$T = 15.32(Q/s)(-0.577 - \ln[r^2S/4Tt]) \quad (1)$$

where

T is aquifer transmissivity, in feet squared per day;

Q/s is specific capacity of the pumped well, in gallons per minute per foot;

r is effective radius of the pumped well, in feet;

S is storage coefficient of the aquifer (dimensionless);

and

t is elapsed pumping time, in days.

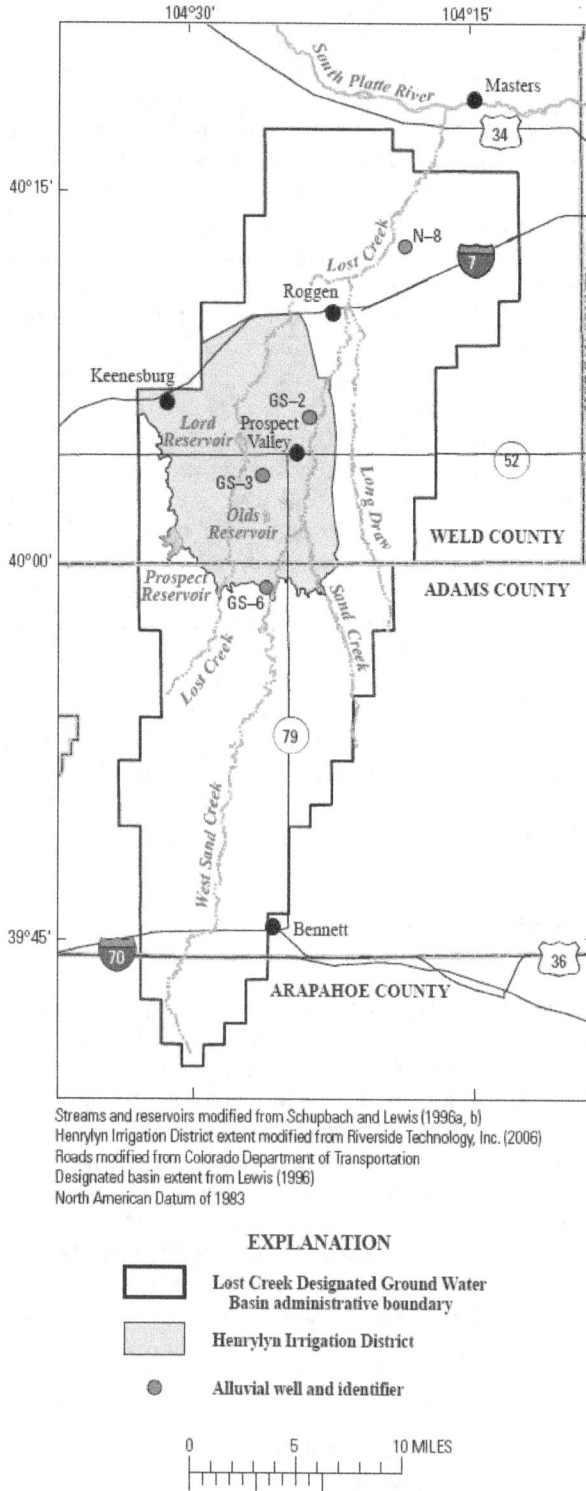

Streams and reservoirs modified from Schupbach and Lewis (1996a, b)
Henrylyn Irrigation District extent modified from Riverside Technology, Inc. (2006)
Roads modified from Colorado Department of Transportation
Designated basin extent from Lewis (1996)
North American Datum of 1983

EXPLANATION

Lost Creek Designated Ground Water
Basin administrative boundary

Henrylyn Irrigation District

● Alluvial well and identifier

0   5   10 MILES

0   5   10 KILOMETERS

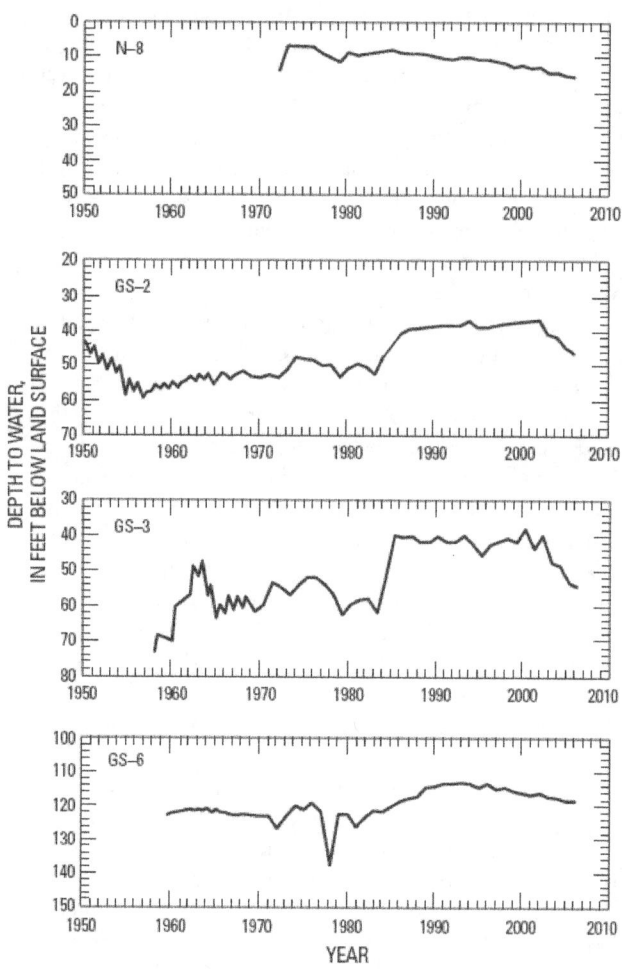

Figure 8. Groundwater levels at selected well locations in the Lost Creek Designated Ground Water Basin, Colorado.

Because aquifer transmissivity (*T*) is on both sides of equation 1, an iterative process was used to solve the equation. Given input values of *Q/s*, *r*, *S*, and *t*, the value of *T* on the left side of the equation was calculated by providing an initial estimate of *T* on the right side of the equation. The calculated value of *T* was then substituted into the right side of the equation, and the process was repeated until the values of *T* on both sides of the equation were essentially the same. Because the alluvial aquifer that constitutes the Lost Creek basin generally is unconfined, the storage coefficient is approximately equal to the specific yield of the aquifer, and specific yield was substituted for *S* in equation 1. Specific yield of sediments in the Lost Creek basin was estimated by Code (1945) to have an average value of about 0.17. Therefore, a specific yield of 0.17 was assumed in calculations of transmissivity using equation 1. Because storage coefficient (*S*) and well radius (*r*) are within the natural-log term of equation 1, calculated transmissivity is relatively insensitive to errors in estimates of *S* and *r*. Transmissivities estimated from the specific capacity of small-diameter wells with small pumping rates typically were found to be an order of magnitude smaller than those estimated from larger-diameter wells with large pumping rates. Therefore, only wells with diameters larger than 16 inches and pumping rates greater than 100 gal/min were used to estimate transmissivity from specific capacity.

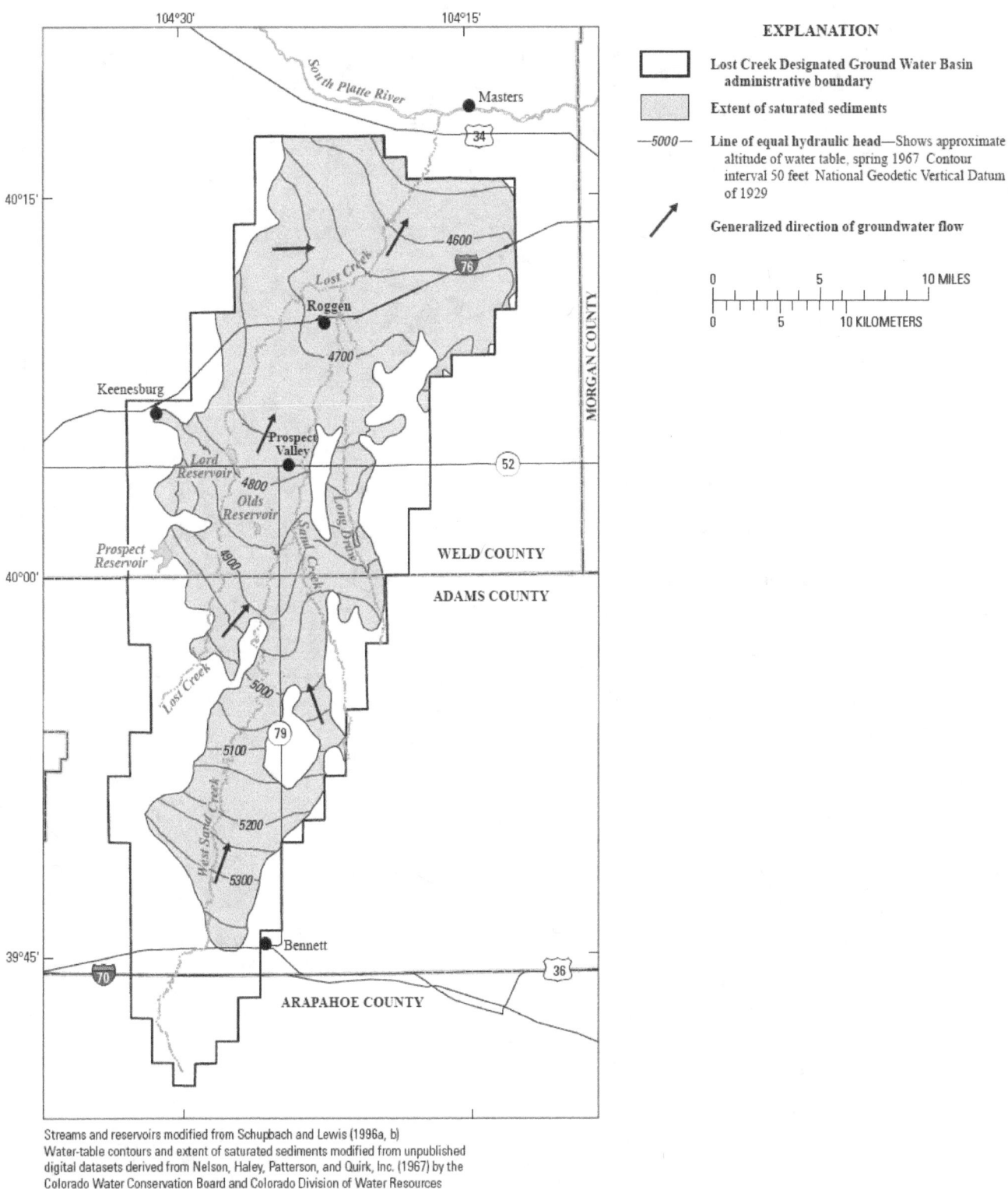

Streams and reservoirs modified from Schupbach and Lewis (1996a, b)
Water-table contours and extent of saturated sediments modified from unpublished
digital datasets derived from Nelson, Haley, Patterson, and Quirk, Inc. (1967) by the
Colorado Water Conservation Board and Colorado Division of Water Resources
Roads modified from Colorado Department of Transportation
Designated basin extent modified from Lewis (1996)
North American Datum of 1983

Figure 9. Generalized configuration of the water table and extent of saturated sediments in the Lost Creek Designated Ground Water Basin, Colorado.

Table 2. Aquifer transmissivity and hydraulic conductivity determined from aquifer tests and estimated from specific capacity of wells in the Lost Creek Designated Ground Water Basin

[CDWR, Colorado Division of Water Resources; USGS, U.S. Geological Survey; (gal/min)/ft, gallons per minute per foot; ft, feet; ft/d, feet per day; ft²/d, feet squared per day]

Well number[1]	Well identifier[2]	Specific capacity [(gal/min)/ft]	Transmissivity value estimated from specific capacity[3] (ft²/d)	Transmissivity value from aquifer test (ft²/d)	Adjusted transmissivity value from power regression[4] (ft²/d)	Saturated thickness[5] (ft)	Estimated hydraulic conductivity (ft/d)	Source
1	NW SW, Sec. 30, T1N, R63W	16	2,900	5,300		60	90	Nelson, Haley, Patterson, and Quirk, Inc. (1967)
2	SW SW, Sec. 35, T2N, R63W	43	8,300	9,000		44	200	Nelson, Haley, Patterson, and Quirk, Inc. (1967)
3	B2-63-26bcc	35	6,500	12,000		59	200	Wilson (1965)
4	Well 5	38	7,100	9,900		48	210	HRS Water Consultants, Inc., written commun. (2006)
5	B2-62-19cd	41	8,600	12,300		48	260	Bjorklund and Brown (1957)
6	Well 6	33	6,100	13,000		51	260	HRS Water Consultants, Inc., written commun. (2006)
7	B2-62-18bca	51	9,800	14,700		55	270	Wilson (1965)
8	Well 2	48	9,200	19,700		71	280	HRS Water Consultants, Inc., written commun. (2006)
9	Well 4	48	9,200	18,300		63	290	HRS Water Consultants, Inc., written commun. (2006)
10	SE SE, Sec. 7, T2N, R62W	44	8,400	13,400		43	310	Nelson, Haley, Patterson, and Quirk, Inc. (1967)
11	B1-63-22acc	71	14,100	30,700		91	340	Wilson (1965)
12	NE SW, Sec. 27, T1N, R63W	61	12,600	26,700		79	340	JR Engineering, written commun. (2005)
13	Well 1	59	11,500	18,300		50	370	HRS Water Consultants, Inc., written commun. (2006)
14	B1-63-9ddc	51	8,650	58,200	3,600	65	900	Skinner (1963)
15	31608FP	15	2,200			40	90	CDWR
16	12474F	20	2,900		4,900	50	100	CDWR
17	12179F	15	2,200		3,600	30	120	CDWR

Table 2. Aquifer transmissivity and hydraulic conductivity determined from aquifer tests and estimated from specific capacity of wells in the Lost Creek Designated Ground Water Basin.—Continued

[CDWR, Colorado Division of Water Resources; USGS, U.S. Geological Survey; (gal/min)/ft, gallons per minute per foot; ft, feet; ft/d, feet per day; ft²/d, feet squared per day]

Well number[1]	Well identifier[2]	Specific capacity [(gal/min)/ft]	Transmissivity value estimated from specific capacity[3] (ft²/d)	Transmissivity value from aquifer test (ft²/d)	Adjusted transmissivity value from power regression[4] (ft²/d)	Saturated thickness[5] (ft)	Estimated hydraulic conductivity (ft/d)	Source
18	175945	19	2,800		4,700	40	120	CDWR
19	31641FP	19	3,000		5,000	40	130	CDWR
20	31605RFP	18	2,500		4,200	30	140	CDWR
21	31607F	24	3,800		6,400	40	160	CDWR
22	9595FPR	31	4,700		8,000	44	180	CDWR
23	18338F	26	4,200		7,000	40	180	CDWR
24	31634F	28	4,200		7,100	40	180	CDWR
25	9598FP	30	4,600		7,700	40	190	CDWR
26	9596FPR	35	5,500		9,400	44	210	CDWR
27	SB00106316AD	64	9,700		16,800	80	210	USGS
28	12172FPR	38	5,900		10,100	44	230	CDWR
29	31604FP	41	5,800		9,900	40	250	CDWR
30	16644FP	41	6,500		11,100	40	280	CDWR
31	17502FP	32	5,200		8,800	30	290	CDWR
32	9594FP	50	7,900		13,500	40	340	CDWR
33	49907F	54	7,900		13,600	40	340	CDWR
34	31635FP	59	9,100		15,700	40	390	CDWR
35	31576F	91	15,300		26,900	65	410	CDWR
36	31555FPR	85	14,500		25,400	36	710	CDWR
37	15719F	100	17,200		30,200	37	820	CDWR

[1] Well number shown in figure 11.

[2] Well identifer for Nelson, Haley, Patterson, and Quirk Inc. (1967) and JR Engineering (written commun., 2005) is well location identifier. Identifer for Wilson (1965) is location number. Identifier for Bjorklund and Brown (1957) and Skinner (1963) is well number. Identifer for CDWR wells is well permit number. Identifier for USGS wells is local well number.

[3] The method of Theis and others (1963, p. 331–341) was used to estimate aquifer transmissivity from specific-capacity data by using a modified form of Theis's equation 1 as presented by Prudic (1991).

[4] Adjusted transmissivity value from power regression determined by relating transmissivity from aquifer tests to transmissivity estimated from specific-capacity at wells for which aquifer-test data were available.

[5] Saturated thickness at wells for which transmissivity was estimated from specific capacity is approximated as the length of the perforated well interval.

Comparison of transmissivities calculated using equation 1 to transmissivities determined from aquifer tests at the same wells indicated that transmissivities estimated from specific capacity were less than those from aquifer tests. Because transmissivity values from aquifer tests are considered more representative than those from specific-capacity tests, transmissivity values estimated from specific-capacity were adjusted on the basis of an equation developed by regressing transmissivity values from 13 of the 14 aquifer tests relative to transmissivity values estimated from specific capacity (fig. 10). Data for one well (B1-63-9ddc) (table 2) was omitted from the regression because the duration of the aquifer test was only 6 hours, and results of the test skewed regression results. The equation used to adjust transmissivities calculated from specific capacity data is:

$$T_{adj} = 1.30 T_{sc}^{1.03} \qquad (2)$$

where

T_{adj} is the final, adjusted transmissivity value, in feet squared per day;

and

T_{sc} is transmissivity estimated from specific capacity, in feet squared per day.

The correlation coefficient of the regression is 0.89, and the coefficient of determination (R^2) is 0.79.

Hydraulic conductivity was estimated by dividing estimated transmissivity by the saturated thickness at each well. Saturated thickness at wells for which transmissivity was estimated from specific capacity was approximated as the length of the perforated well interval. The hydraulic-conductivity distribution and location of wells used to estimate hydraulic conductivity are shown in figure 11. The locations and values of aquifer-test and specific-capacity data also are available as a Geographic Information System dataset (Arnold, 2010) at *http://water.usgs.gov/lookup/getgislist*. Data from aquifer tests

and specific-capacity estimates indicate hydraulic conductivity ranges from 90 to 900 ft/d with most values ranging from about 100 to 400 ft/d (table 2). Hydraulic conductivity generally is largest near the middle of the Lost Creek basin, where the deepest part of the paleovalley is located, and hydraulic conductivity generally decreases toward the basin margins. Although hydraulic-conductivity estimates were not available for sediments near the basin margins, hydraulic conductivity in these areas likely is less than 100 ft/d based on the generally higher clay content of sediments in these areas. Although eolian sands cover much of the study area (fig. 5), these deposits generally do not extend below the water table. For this reason, surface geology was not used to guide the hydraulic-conductivity distribution of the aquifer. Average hydraulic-conductivity values of bedrock aquifers (Denver, Arapahoe, and Laramie–Fox Hills) underlying the Lost Creek basin ranges from 0.5 to 2 ft/d (Robson, 1983, sheet 1), which is about 2 orders of magnitude less than the hydraulic conductivity of most alluvium in the Lost Creek basin.

Recharge

Recharge to the Lost Creek basin primarily occurs as (1) infiltration of precipitation, (2) infiltration of ephemeral stream water, (3) deep percolation of water applied to irrigated agricultural fields, and (4) seepage beneath irrigation ditches and reservoirs. Septic-system return flow of water withdrawn by low-capacity domestic wells completed in the Denver Basin bedrock aquifers underlying the Lost Creek basin also likely contributes a small amount of recharge to the basin, but recharge from domestic septic systems is not explicitly considered by this study. Depending on the hydraulic gradient between the alluvial aquifer of the Lost Creek basin and the underlying bedrock aquifers, the Lost Creek basin also may receive groundwater inflow directly from the bedrock aquifers. However, because the hydraulic conductivity of the bedrock aquifers is much smaller than that of the alluvial aquifer, inflow from the bedrock aquifers likely is small compared to recharge from other sources. Estimation of groundwater inflow to the Lost Creek basin from bedrock aquifers is beyond the scope of this report.

Precipitation Infiltration

Recharge from infiltration of precipitation on native grassland and nonirrigated agricultural fields in the Lost Creek basin was estimated for this study by using the chloride mass-balance method (CMB). The CMB method uses the concentration of chloride in soil profiles to estimate the flux of water from land surface to the water table. The CMB method has been used in several previous studies (Allison and Hughes, 1978; Allison and others, 1994; Roark and Healy, 1998; Maurer and Thodal, 2000; McMahon and others, 2003; Stonestrom and others, 2003) to estimate aquifer recharge. Chloride profiles develop in soil as water containing small quantities of chloride infiltrates into the

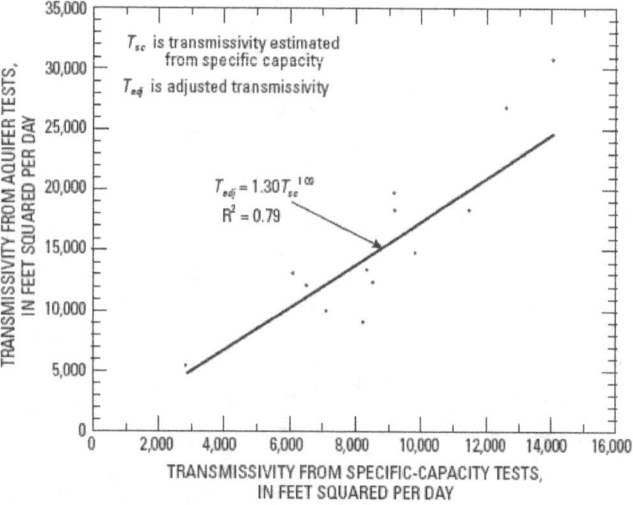

Figure 10.   Relation of transmissivity determined from aquifer tests to transmissivity estimated from specific-capacity tests for 13 wells in the Lost Creek Designated Ground Water Basin.

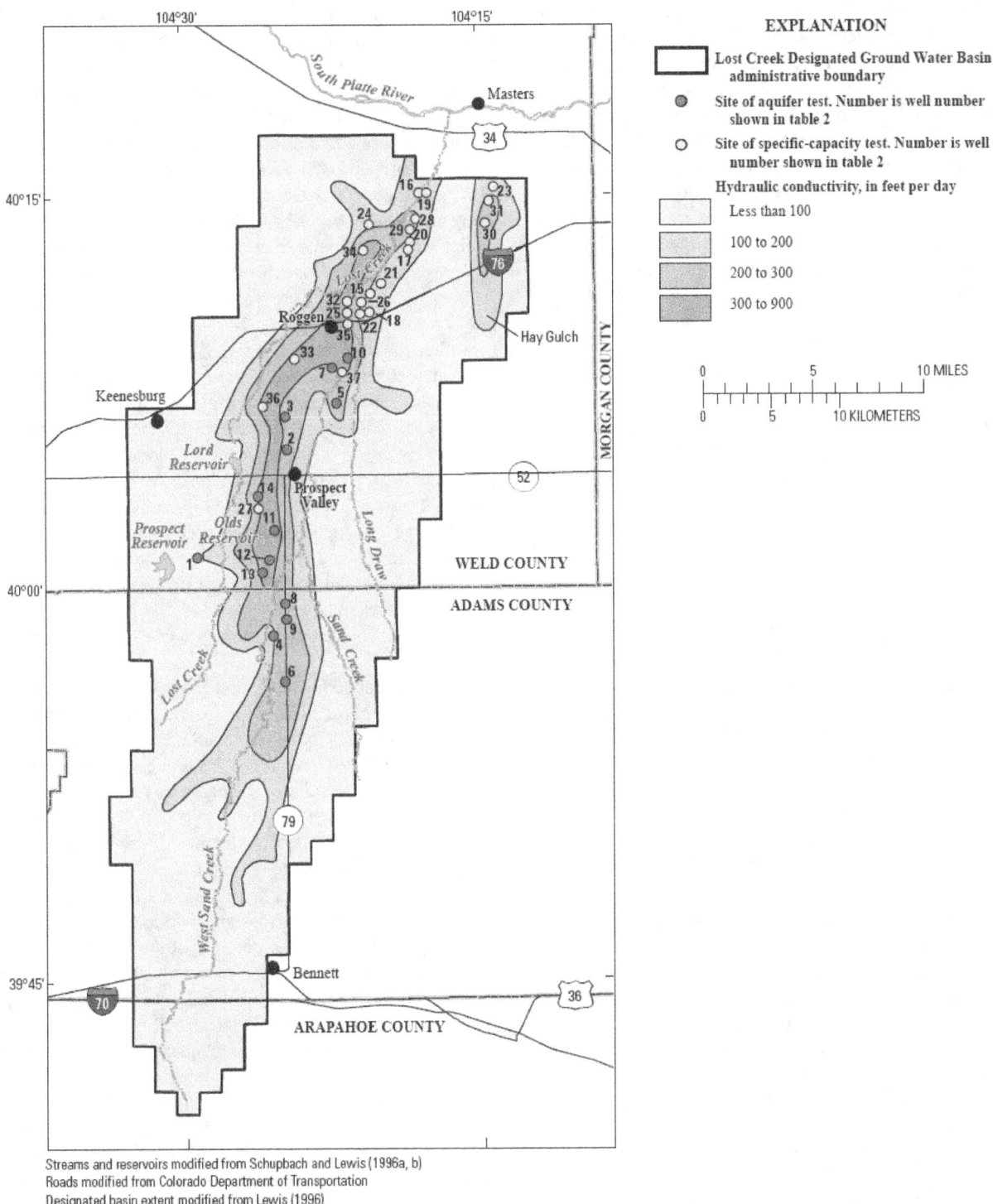

Streams and reservoirs modified from Schupbach and Lewis (1996a, b)
Roads modified from Colorado Department of Transportation
Designated basin extent modified from Lewis (1996)
North American Datum of 1983

Figure 11. Hydraulic-conductivity distribution and location of aquifer tests and specific-capacity tests used to estimate hydraulic conductivity in the Lost Creek Designated Ground Water Basin, Colorado.

ground. For nonirrigated areas, the chloride concentration in the infiltrating water represents the sum of chloride in precipitation (wetfall) and aerosols (dryfall). For irrigated areas, chloride in the applied irrigation water also contributes to the chloride concentration of the infiltrating water. As water is removed from the soil profile by evapotranspiration, chloride accumulates in the root zone. Under true steady-state conditions, the chloride concentration in the soil profile is expected to increase gradually from land surface to a maximum concentration near a depth not affected by evapotranspiration (Wood, 1999). The exact depth at which maximum chloride concentration (chloride peak) occurs is a function of climate, soil texture, vegetation root depth, and other factors. Between the point of maximum chloride concentration and the water table, the chloride concentration is expected to be relatively constant because water infiltrating below this depth is not affected by evapotranspiration. If water infiltrating below the depth of effective evapotranspiration is assumed to flow to the aquifer, the chloride concentration in soil water below this depth can be related to the recharge rate (q_w) using the equation (Allison and others, 1994):

$$q_w = (C_p P)/C_s \qquad (3)$$

where

q_w is the recharge rate, in inches per year;

C_p is the effective chloride concentration in precipitation (wetfall plus dryfall), in milligrams per liter;

P is the rate of precipitation, in inches per year;

and

C_s is the average chloride concentration in soil water below the depth of effective evapotranspiration, in milligrams per liter.

Assumptions made in application of equation 3 are that (1) land surface is neither aggrading nor degrading, (2) atmospheric deposition (wetfall plus dryfall) is the only chloride source and is constant through time, (3) the chloride moves steadily and uniformly downward with the infiltrating water, and (4) soil-water chloride concentrations are in equilibrium with chloride flux at the land surface. Important sources of uncertainty in estimating recharge rates by using equation 3 are the chloride concentration in precipitation and the selection of appropriate depths to represent steady-state water flux in the unsaturated zone, which is subject to interpretation and therefore has inherent uncertainty that cannot be quantified.

Long-term average recharge rates from precipitation were estimated for four sites (fig. 12) in the Lost Creek basin by using the CMB method. Sites C1 and C4 are located in native grassland areas, and sites C3 and C5 are located in nonirrigated agricultural fields. Sites in nonirrigated agricultural fields were selected where fertilizers containing chloride were not known to have been applied. Soil samples were collected at each site in 2-ft intervals to a depth of 20 ft below land surface by using a hand-driven

bucket auger, and samples immediately were placed in soil tins and sealed with plastic tape to preserve soil moisture. Laboratory measurements of gravimetric water content and chloride concentration were completed for each sample at the USGS National Research Program laboratory in Lakewood, Colorado. Gravimetric water content was determined by measuring the weight of soil samples before and after oven drying using methods described by Dane and Topp (2002). Chloride concentrations were determined using methods described by McMahon and others (2003). As a brief description of the process used, air-dried sediment was mixed with deionized water in a 1:10 (sediment:water) mass ratio. After mixing, samples were placed on an orbital shaker for 1 hour at 170 revolutions per minute. The samples were then spun in a centrifuge for 10 minutes, after which water was extracted and passed through a 0.45-µm filter. Chloride concentrations in the filtered solution were quantified using ion chromatography. Gravimetric water content and chloride concentrations determined for each site are presented in Appendix 1. Chloride data were quality assured by analyzing deionized water or a method blank generally after about every third field sample to assess contamination and by analyzing 2–4 duplicate samples per site to assess analytical precision (Appendix 2). Lithologic logs of soils at each site are presented in figure 13. Profiles of chloride concentrations at each site are presented in figure 14.

Chloride concentrations in wet plus dry deposition were estimated from data (Appendix 3) collected at the Pawnee National Atmospheric Deposition Program (NADP) site (fig. 2) located about 40 mi north of the Lost Creek basin, where climatic and physiographic conditions are similar to those in the Lost Creek basin. Estimates of wet deposition in the Lost Creek basin are based on data collected at the Pawnee site from 1979 to 2004 (National Atmospheric Deposition Program, 2005). Estimates of dry deposition in the Lost Creek basin are based on unpublished data collected at the Pawnee site from 1979 to 1990 (Robert Larson, National Atmospheric Deposition Program, written commun., 2006). The average effective chloride concentration in precipitation (0.13 mg/L) at the Pawnee site represents the sum of average wet and dry deposition rates, divided by the average precipitation rate. Average recharge rates (table 3) at sites in the Lost Creek basin were estimated using equation 3 with the average effective chloride concentration in precipitation at the Pawnee site, the average long-term precipitation rate (14.1 in/yr) in the Lost Creek basin, and chloride concentrations of soil water collected at each site. The sample depths used to calculate the average chloride concentration in soil water were selected to represent steady-state flux of water through the unsaturated zone. In cases where a single chloride peak occurred near the top of the soil profile (sites C1 and C5), the average chloride concentration of soil water in the interval of relatively uniform values below the peak was used to calculate recharge using equation 3. In cases where a chloride peak appears to have been flushed downward (sites C3 and C4), the average chloride concentration of soil water above, between, and below the peak(s) was used to calculate recharge by using equation 3.

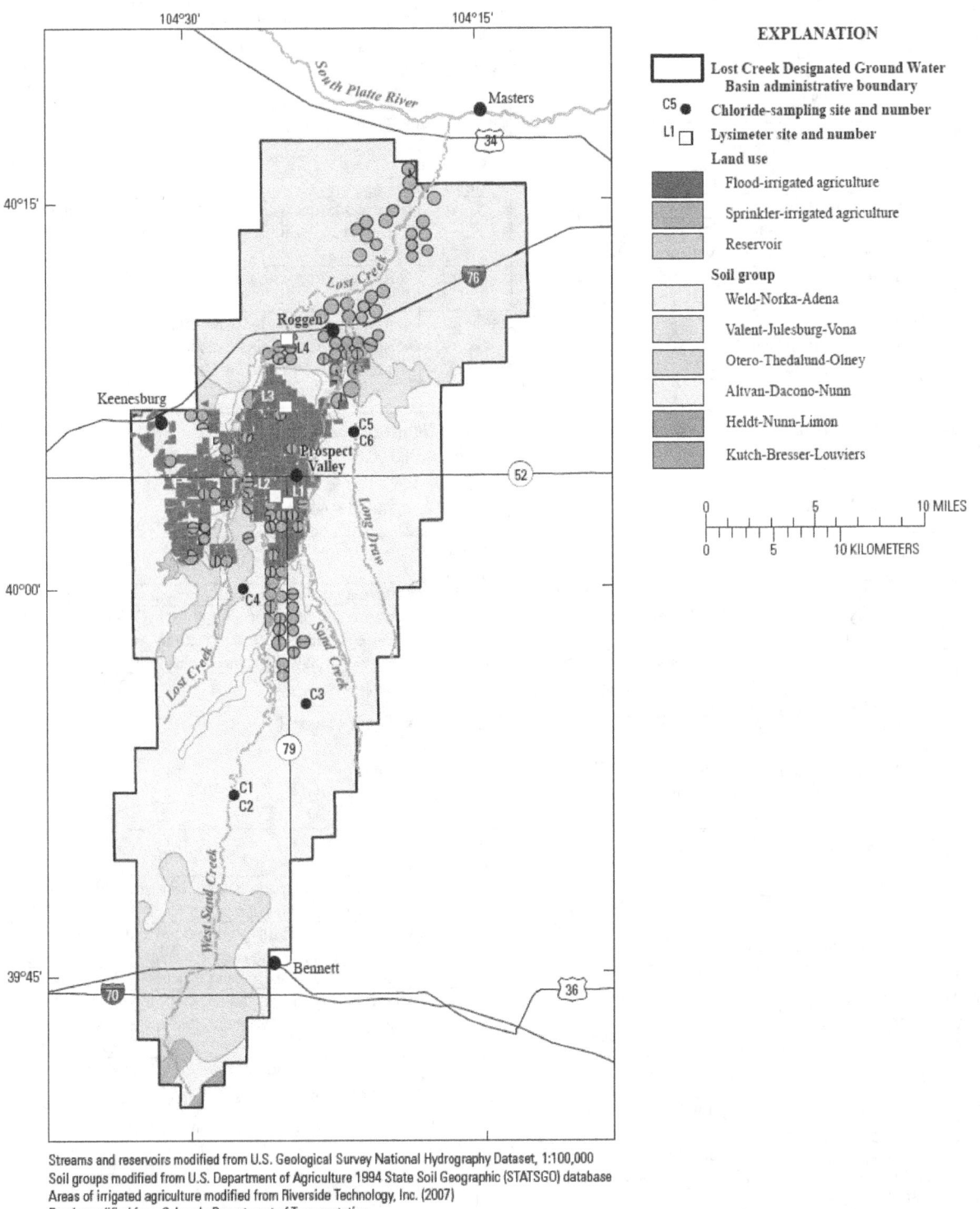

EXPLANATION

☐ Lost Creek Designated Ground Water
   Basin administrative boundary

C5 ● Chloride-sampling site and number

L1 ☐ Lysimeter site and number

Land use

   Flood-irrigated agriculture

   Sprinkler-irrigated agriculture

   Reservoir

Soil group

   Weld-Norka-Adena

   Valent-Julesburg-Vona

   Otero-Thedalund-Olney

   Altvan-Dacono-Nunn

   Heldt-Nunn-Limon

   Kutch-Bresser-Louviers

Streams and reservoirs modified from U.S. Geological Survey National Hydrography Dataset, 1:100,000
Soil groups modified from U.S. Department of Agriculture 1994 State Soil Geographic (STATSGO) database
Areas of irrigated agriculture modified from Riverside Technology, Inc. (2007)
Roads modified from Colorado Department of Transportation
Designated basin extent modified from Lewis (1996)
North American Datum of 1983

Figure 12.   Location of chloride-sampling sites and passive-wick lysimeters used for estimation of recharge beneath native grassland, nonirrigated agricultural fields, irrigated agricultural fields, and ephemeral stream channels in the Lost Creek Designated Ground Water Basin, Colorado.

Site C1 - Native grassland
Latitude: 39°52'01.8"
Longitude: 104°27'41.0"
Land-surface altitude: 5,223 feet

Depth (feet)	Description
0–0.7	Clayey fine sand, dark brown, frozen
0.7–2.5	Clayey fine sand, light brown, moist
2.5–5	Clayey fine sand, grayish tan, dry
5–16	Well-graded sand, fine to coarse with minor gravel, subangular to subrounded, slightly clayey in lenses, light brown, dry 5–10 ft, damp 10–11 ft, moist 11–16 ft
16–20	Clay, slightly sandy to sandy, clayey sand lens from 19–19.5 ft, light brown, moist

Site C2 - West Sand Creek channel
Latitude: 39°52'01.7"
Longitude: 104°27'42.4"
Land-surface altitude: 5,218 feet

Depth (feet)	Description
0–5	Sand, fine to coarse, subangular to subrounded, light brown, dry 0–0.5 ft, damp 0.5–1ft, moist 1–4.5 ft, wet 4.5–5 ft
5–6.8	Sand, fine to coarse, subangular to subrounded, slightly gravelly, slightly clayey to clayey, light brown, wet
6.8–7	Clay, slightly sandy, light brown, moist
7–9	Sand, fine with minor medium, subangular to subrounded, silty, tan, moist
9–15	Silty clay, sandy in lenses, light brown, moist
15–17.5	Sand, fine, subangular to subrounded, silty to clayey, tan, moist
17.5–19	Clay, light brown, moist
19–20	Sand, fine, subangular to subrounded, silty to clayey, tan, moist

Site C3 - Nonirrigated agricultural field
Latitude: 39°55'35.0"
Longitude: 104°23'59.5"
Land-surface altitude: 5,115 feet

Depth (feet)	Description
0–7	Clayey silt with very fine sand, light brown, moist 0–2 ft, damp 2–7 ft
7–14	Silty clayey sand, very fine to fine, contains caliche and minor coarse material, reddish brown 7–9 ft, light brown 9–14 ft, damp to moist
14–15.5	Silty fine sand, slightly clayey with caliche, tan, damp
15.5–17	Silty clayey sand, very fine to fine, contains caliche and minor coarse material, reddish brown to light brown, damp to moist
17–20	Sand, fine to coarse, subangular to subrounded, slightly gravelly, tan, damp

Site C4 - Native grassland (previously nonirrigated agricultural field)
Latitude: 40°00'03.0"
Longitude: 104°27'06.9"
Land-surface altitude: 4,971 feet

Depth (feet)	Description
0–7	Silty sand, fine with minor coarse, slightly clayey to clayey, light brown 0–2.5 ft, tan with caliche 2.5–7 ft
7–9.5	Silty sand, fine with minor coarse and gravel, tan, dry to damp
9.5–20	Clayey silty sand, fine with minor medium to coarse and gravel, contains caliche, light brown to tan, damp 9.5–19 ft, moist 19–20 ft

Site C5 - Nonirrigated agricultural field
Latitude: 40°06'06.2"
Longitude: 104°21'24.4"
Land-surface altitude: 4,770 feet

Depth (feet)	Description
0–2	Silty, clayey fine sand, dark brown, damp to moist
2–19	Silty, clayey fine sand, light brown 2–9 ft, dark brown 9–10 ft and 15.5 to 19 ft, dry to damp
19–20	Sandy, silty clay, contains caliche, grayish-brown, damp

Site C6 - Long Draw channel
Latitude: 40°06'06.3"
Longitude: 104°21'23.5"
Land-surface altitude: 4,766 feet

Depth (feet)	Description
0–5	Silty clay, slightly sandy, dark brown and damp 0–2 ft, brown and dry to damp 2–5 ft
5–13.5	Clayey fine sand, silty, light brown and damp to moist 5–13.5 ft, brown to dark brown and moist 13.5–15 ft
13.5–15	Silty clay with fine sand and caliche, light grayish-brown
15–19.8	Clayey silt with fine sand to clayey, silty sand, light grayish-brown with abundant rust staining, damp to moist
19.8–20	Silty sand, fine with minor medium and coarse, tan with rust staining, damp

Latitude and longitude referenced to the North American Datum of 1983
Land-surface altitude referenced to the National Geodetic Vertical Datum of 1929

Figure 13. Lithologic descriptions of soils at chloride-sampling sites used to estimate recharge beneath native grassland, nonirrigated agricultural fields, and ephemeral stream channels in the Lost Creek Designated Ground Water Basin, Colorado.

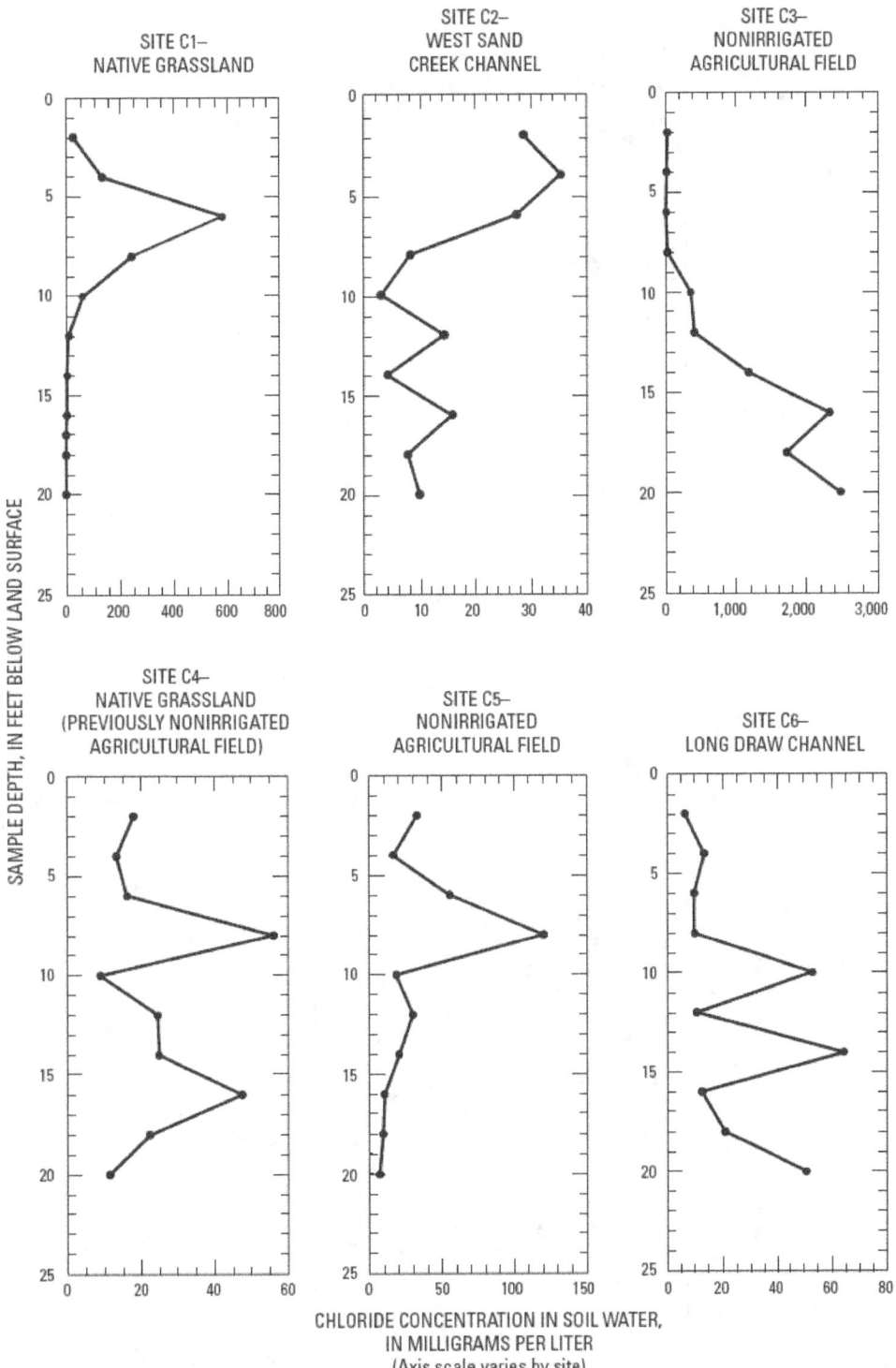

Figure 14. Vertical profiles of chloride concentrations in soil water beneath native grassland, nonirrigated agricultural fields, and ephemeral stream channels in the Lost Creek Designated Ground Water Basin, Colorado.

Table 3. Chloride concentration of soil water and precipitation, rate of precipitation, and recharge rates estimated from soil-chloride profiles beneath native grassland, nonirrigated agricultural fields, and ephemeral stream channels in the Lost Creek Designated Ground Water Basin.

[ft, feet; mg/L, milligrams per liter; g/g, gram water per gram soil; cm³/cm³, cubic centimeter water per cubic centimeter soil; in/yr, inches per year; –, no data]

Site	Site description	Depth interval(s)[1] (ft)	Average chloride concentration of soil water[2] (mg/L)	Average effective chloride concentration of precipitation[3] (mg/L)	Average annual precipitation (inches)	Average gravimetric water content[2] (g/g)	Average volumetric water content[4] (cm³/cm³)	Apparent displacement velocity of chloride peak[5] (in/yr)	Estimated average annual recharge[6] (inches)
C1	Native grassland	14–20	3.24	0.13	14.1	0.17	0.29	–	0.6
C2	West Sand Creek channel	4–12	–	–	–	0.15	0.26	32	8.2
C2	West Sand Creek channel	12–16	–	–	–	0.24	0.41	16	6.5
C3	Nonirrigated agricultural field	2–8	22.2	0.13	14.1	0.17	0.29	–	0.1
C4	Native grassland/nonirrigated agricultural field	10, 20	10.3	0.13	14.1	0.20	0.34	–	0.2
C5	Nonirrigated agricultural field	16–20	8.75	0.13	14.1	0.22	0.37	–	0.2
C6	Long Draw channel	4–10	–	–	–	0.15	0.26	24	6.1
C6	Long Draw channel	10–14	–	–	–	0.21	0.36	16	5.7
C6	Long Draw channel	14–20	–	–	–	0.20	0.34	24	8.2

[1]Depth intervals referenced to land surface.

[2]Average chloride concentration of soil water and average gravimetric moisture content are the arithmetic averages of all samples in depth interval(s) indicated.

[3]Average effective chloride concentration of precipitation represents the sum of average wet and dry deposition rates, divided by the average precipitation rate, during 1979–2004 at the Pawnee National Atmospheric Deposition Program site.

[4]Average volumetric water content is calculated as average gravimetric water content multiplied by an assumed soil bulk density of 1.70 grams per cubic centimeter and divided by a water density of 1 gram per cubic centimeter.

[5]Average displacement velocity of chloride peak calculated as depth interval in inches divided by an assumed traveltime (streamflow frequency) of 3 years.

[6]Average annual recharge at sites C1, C3, C4, and C5 estimated by using the chloride mass-balance method. Average annual recharge at sites C2 and C6 estimated by using the apparent displacement velocity of chloride peaks as presented by Stonestrom and others (2003).

The chloride profile (fig. 14) at site C1 (native grassland) has a peak chloride concentration of 592 mg/L at a depth 6 ft below land surface (Appendix 1), and chloride concentrations decrease below the peak to relatively uniform values in the interval from 14 to 20 ft with an average value of 3.24 mg/L (table 3). The single chloride peak near land surface likely represents the accumulation of chloride by evapotranspiration just below the root zone, and the relatively uniform chloride concentrations below the peak indicates the recharge rate at site C1 likely has been relatively stable over time. Average annual recharge at site C1 is estimated by using equation 3 to be about 0.6 inch based on the average chloride concentration in soil water from 14 to 20 ft below land surface.

At the time of sampling (2006), site C4 was located in native grassland; however, a local landowner reported that site C4 previously was used for nonirrigated agriculture several (unspecified) years prior to sampling. The chloride profile (fig. 14) at site C4 has two distinct chloride concentration peaks. The first peak has a chloride concentration of 56.1 mg/L at a depth of 8 ft (Appendix 1), and the second peak has a chloride concentration of 47.6 mg/L at a depth of 16 ft. The average chloride concentration of soil water in the intervals between (10-ft depth) and below (20-ft depth) the chloride peaks is 10.3 mg/L (table 3). The presence of two peaks in the chloride profile at site C4 may be the result of changing land use and vegetation at the site. The chloride peak at a depth of 8 ft, which has a depth similar to that beneath native grassland at site C1, may have developed under current native grassland conditions at the site, whereas the chloride peak at a depth of 16 ft may represent chloride that accumulated under native conditions prior to using the site for nonirrigated agriculture and was subsequently flushed downward when the site was converted to nonirrigated agriculture. Average annual recharge at site C4 is estimated by using equation 3 to be about 0.2 inch based on the average chloride concentration of soil water at depths of 10 and 20 ft below land surface.

Chloride concentrations in soil water at site C3 (non-irrigated agricultural field) are relatively uniform in the interval from 2 to 8 ft below land surface (fig. 14) with an average value of 22.2 mg/L (table 3) and increase to a peak value of 2,480 mg/L at a depth of 20 ft below land surface (Appendix 1). The peak chloride concentration at a depth of 20 ft may represent flushing of root-zone accumulated chloride to greater depth. Because the relatively uniform chloride concentrations from 2 to 8 ft appear to represent steady-state conditions, the average chloride concentration of soil water in the interval from 2 to 8 ft was used to estimate recharge at site C3. Average annual recharge at site C3 is estimated by using equation 3 to be about 0.1 inch based on the average chloride concentration of soil water from 2 to 8 ft below land surface.

The chloride profile (fig. 14) at site C5 (nonirrigated agricultural field) has a peak chloride concentration of 120 mg/L at a depth 8 ft below land surface (Appendix 1), and chloride concentrations decrease below the peak to relatively uniform values in the interval from 16 to 20 ft with an average value of 8.75 mg/L (table 3). The depth of the peak chloride concentration at site C5 is similar to the depth of the peak at site C1 and the upper peak at site C4, indicating that the chloride peak at site C5 represents the accumulation of chloride by evapotranspiration just below the root zone. Similar to site C1, the relatively uniform chloride concentrations below the peak also indicates the recharge rate at site C5 has been relatively stable over time. Average annual recharge at site C5 is estimated by using equation 3 to be about 0.2 inch based on the average chloride concentrations in the interval from 16 to 20 ft.

Additional chloride profiles distributed throughout the Lost Creek basin would be useful for verifying recharge estimates and providing estimates of basin-scale recharge. However, estimates of recharge beneath native grassland and nonirrigated agricultural fields are reasonably consistent (0.1–0.6 in/yr) among the sites analyzed and are within the range (0.008–1.4 inches) reported for recharge in semiarid and arid regions worldwide (Scanlon and others, 2006). Estimated recharge beneath native grassland and nonirrigated agricultural fields in the Lost Creek basin represents about 1–4 percent of long-term average precipitation (14.1 inch).

Stream-Channel Infiltration

Recharge from stream-channel infiltration is dependent on the thickness and hydraulic properties of sediments underlying the stream channel, streambed geomorphology, runoff characteristics of the contributing drainage basin, and the availability of streamflow (Coes and Pool, 2005). Recharge from infiltration of ephemeral streamflow in the Lost Creek basin was estimated for this study by using the concentration of chloride in soil profiles beneath West Sand Creek (site C2; fig. 12) and Long Draw (site C6). Because the volume and chloride concentration of streamflow in West Sand Creek and Long Draw are unknown, recharge beneath ephemeral stream channels was estimated by using apparent downward velocities of chloride peaks in the profiles rather than using the CMB method. Recharge can be estimated from apparent travel velocities of chloride peaks by using the equation (Stonestrom and others, 2003):

$$q_w = \theta(z_2 - z_1)/(t_2 - t_1) \qquad (4)$$

where

q_w is the recharge rate, in inches per year;

θ is the average volumetric water content in the interval traveled by the chloride peak (dimensionless);

$(z_2 - z_1)$ is the vertical distance traveled by the chloride peak, in inches;

and

$(t_2 - t_1)$ is the elapsed time of chloride peak movement, in years.

Application of equation 4 assumes that chloride moves conservatively downward with infiltrating water and that the volumetric water content between chloride peaks is constant through time. Assumptions about the timing and frequency of flow in stream channels is an important source of uncertainty in the application of equation 4 to estimation of stream-channel infiltration in the Lost Creek basin.

Chloride profiles at sites C2 and C6 have multiple chloride peaks (fig. 14) to the depths sampled, which may indicate periodic flushing of chloride that accumulated in the root zone between stormflow events. The peak chloride concentrations generally are less than at other sites, indicating that chloride had less time to accumulate in the root zone before being flushed downward by the next stormflow event. Peak chloride concentrations at site C2 occur at depths of 4 ft (35.3 mg/L), 12 ft (14.4 mg/L), and 16 ft (15.8 mg/L) (Appendix 1), and peak chloride concentrations occur at site C6 at depths of 4 ft (13.4 mg/L), 10 ft (53.0 mg/L), 14 ft (64.5 mg/L), and 20 ft (50.7 mg/L). The uppermost chloride peak at a depth of 4 ft at site C2 and the slightly elevated chloride concentration at a depth of 4 ft at site C6 may represent the accumulation of chloride in the root zone since the most recent stormflow event. Assuming deeper chloride peaks also initially developed in the root zone at a depth of 4 ft, the vertical distance between successive peaks provides an indication of the distance traveled by the peaks. Using the vertical distance between successive peaks ($z_2 - z_1$), the average volumetric water content in the interval between successive peaks (θ), and an assumed streamflow frequency ($t_2 - t_1$) of once every 3 years (see "Physiography and Climate"), average annual recharge at site C2 (West Sand Creek) is estimated by using equation 4 to range from about 6.5 to 8.2 inches (table 3) with an average value of 7.4 inches. Similarly, average annual recharge at site C6 (Long Draw) is estimated by using equation 4 to range from about 5.7 to 8.2 inches with an average value of 6.7 inches. Although infiltration below ephemeral stream channels occurs only infrequently and is confined to narrow areas, available streamflow generally infiltrates rapidly below the depth of effective evapotranspiration, and water that infiltrates below ephemeral stream channels likely contributes recharge to the Lost Creek basin.

Deep Percolation of Water Applied to Irrigated Agricultural Fields

Recharge from deep percolation of water applied to irrigated agricultural fields was estimated for this study by using passive-wick lysimeters to measure subsurface drainage beneath irrigated fields during the 2007 and 2008 irrigation seasons and by a water-balance method. Although the CMB method has been used to estimate recharge beneath irrigated agricultural fields by other studies (Roark and Healy, 1998; Maurer and Thodal, 2000; Stonestrom and

others, 2003), passive-wick lysimeters, rather than the CMB method, was the primary method used to estimate recharge beneath irrigated agricultural fields in this study because of uncertainties associated with the concentration of chloride in irrigation water and fertilizer applied to irrigated agricultural fields in the Lost Creek basin. Recharge also was estimated by using a water-balance method to provide for comparison of the two methods. Although recharge estimated by lysimeter drainage might not represent long-term steady-state conditions, lysimeter-drainage data were used to estimate recharge because other data concerning recharge beneath irrigated fields were lacking. Additional data concerning recharge beneath irrigated fields would be important to improving estimates of long-term average recharge rates beneath irrigated fields in the Lost Creek basin.

Passive-Wick Lysimeters

Passive-wick lysimeters were installed at four sites (fig. 12) in the Lost Creek basin. Sites were selected to represent different irrigation methods and major soil types within the basin to provide for comparison of recharge under different conditions. Sites L1 and L4 are located in agricultural fields irrigated by center-pivot sprinkler systems. Sites L2 and L3 are located in fields irrigated by using flood furrows. All four sites were irrigated with groundwater. Sites L1, L2, and L3 are located in loam soils of the Weld-Norka-Adena group. Site L4 is located in sandy soils of the Valent-Julesburg-Vona group. Deep percolation beneath a flood-irrigated field overlying sandy soils of the Valent-Julesburg-Vona group was not measured because flood-irrigated fields generally are not present on this soil group in the Lost Creek basin.

Each passive-wick lysimeter consists of a 26-inch-long, 7.9-inch-diameter, soil-filled metal cylinder (divergence-control tube; DCT) mounted above a collector plate that funnels percolating water into a small measurement chamber monitored by a water-depth sensor (fig. 15). When the water level in the measurement chamber reaches the top of a siphon tube, the water drains from the measurement chamber, and the volume of water drained is recorded by a data logger. Capillary suction is maintained in the lysimeter by a fiberglass wick that extends between the collector plate and the measurement chamber to passively drain the lysimeter (Gee and others, 2002). The DCT is designed to minimize divergence of water around the lysimeter so that measured drainage is representative of percolation outside the lysimeter.

Lysimeters were installed by excavating a small 2-ft-deep pit within the irrigated area of each field and driving the DCT into soils at the bottom of the pit in order to fill the tube with relatively undisturbed soil representative of in-situ soil layers at the site (fig. 15). The soil-filled DCT was then extracted and installed along with other components of the lysimeter adjacent to and at the same depth as the core-sample location. The pit was backfilled in compacted layers with soil excavated

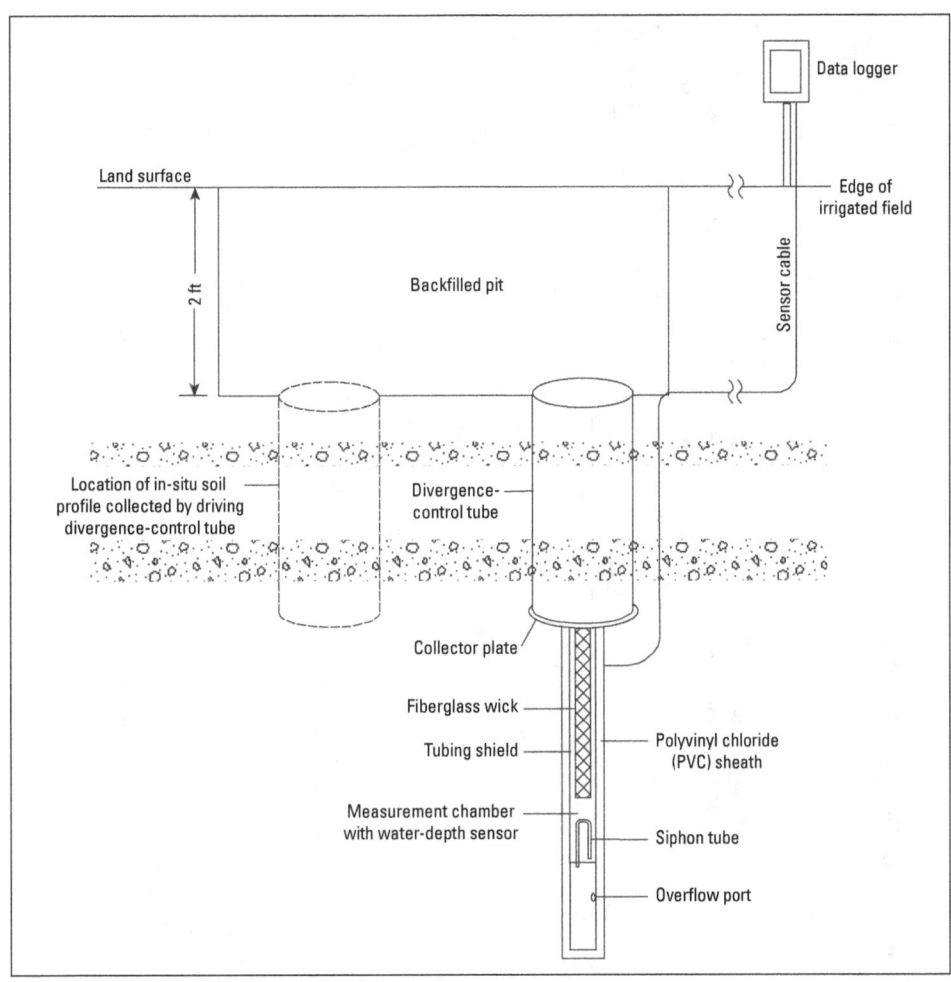

NOT TO SCALE

Figure 15.   Passive-wick lysimeter design and installation.

from the pit to restore soil as nearly as possible to in-situ conditions, and any vegetation was replaced at land surface. The top of the DCT was installed about 2 ft below land surface to enable farming practices, such as plowing or tilling, to be conducted normally without interference by the lysimeter and to maintain representative field conditions. The collector plate at the base of the DCT was located about 4 ft below land surface at a depth generally below substantial root development. Each lysimeter was connected to an automated data logger installed at the outside edge of the irrigated field by means of a buried cable, and the volume of drainage through the lysimeter was recorded. Small tipping-bucket rain gages were installed within the irrigated area of each sprinkler site (sites L1 and L4) to record the volume of applied water for comparison to farmer's irrigation records.

Daily net irrigation, precipitation, crop evapotranspiration, and lysimeter-drainage data for each site are presented in Appendix 4, and total values for each period of analysis are shown in table 4. Data were collected for parts of the 2007 and 2008 irrigation seasons. The period of analysis generally is from the first irrigation event to 15 days after the last irrigation event in each season. However, the period of analysis in 2008 for site L1 ends only 6 days after an irrigation event because irrigation continued at the site beyond the end of the study period. A period of 15 days after the last irrigation event is used to allow time for any water stored in the unsaturated zone above the lysimeter to percolate downward to the lysimeter.

Net irrigation of sprinkler-irrigated fields (sites L1 and L4) was estimated based on farmer application records and verified by data from rain gages installed within the irrigated area. Net irrigation of flood-irrigated fields (sites L2 and L3) was estimated as the total volume of water pumped to the field minus assumed runoff, divided by the number of irrigated acres. The total volume of water applied to fields was determined by multiplying the estimated well-pumping rate by the estimated pumping duration based on farmers' records. Based on observations during irrigation events and discussions with farmers, runoff was assumed to be 10 percent of total applied

Table 4. Net irrigation, precipitation, crop consumptive use, and recharge estimated by lysimeter drainage and a water-balance method for four irrigated agricultural fields in the Lost Creek Designated Ground Water Basin.

[–, no data]

Site	Period[1]	Irrigation method	Soil type[2]	Crop type	Net irrigation[3] (inches)	Precipitation[4] (inches)	Crop evapotranspiration[5] (inches)	Recharge estimated by lysimeter drainage[6] (inches)	Recharge estimated by water balance[7] (inches)	Ratio of recharge estimated by lysimeter drainage to net irrigation (percent)	Ratio of recharge estimated by lysimeter drainage to net irrigation plus precipitation (percent)	Ratio of recharge estimated by water balance to net irrigation (percent)	Ratio of recharge estimated by water balance to net irrigation plus precipitation (percent)
L1	6/3–10/20/07	Center-pivot sprinkler	Loam	Alfalfa	19.4	5.7	30.5	1.0	0.0	5	4	0	0
L1	4/8–9/17/08			Alfalfa	26.6	5.1	26.7	1.8	5.0	7	6	19	16
L2	5/19–6/15/07	Flood furrow	Loam	Wheat	0.5	1.5	8.2	0.1	0.0	20	5	0	0
L2	5/20–9/17/08			Corn	–	–	–	–	–	–	–	–	–
L3	6/22–9/14/07	Flood furrow	Loam	Corn	26.0	4.6	19.3	3.5	11.3	13	11	43	37
L3	6/28–9/1/08			Sunflowers	–	–	–	–	–	–	–	–	–
L4	6/30–10/5/07	Center-pivot sprinkler	Sand	Corn	13.1	4.5	19.9	3.0	0.0	23	17	0	0
L4	5/8–9/30/08			Alfalfa	13.2	2.2	17.1	4.0	0.0	30	26	0	0
	Average sprinkler		Loam					1.4	2.5	6	5	10	8
	Average sprinkler		Sand					3.5	0.0	27	22	0	0
	Average flood furrow		Loam					1.8	5.7	17	8	22	19

[1]Period is from first irrigation event over lysimeter to 15 days after last irrigation event over lysimeter or the end of the study on September 30, 2008.

[2]Soil type from Heil and others (1978).

[3]Net irrigation of flood fields is calculated as the difference between the total volume of water pumped onto the field minus estimated runoff, divided by the number of irrigated acres. Pumping data were provided by farmers. Net irrigation of sprinkler fields is estimated based on farmer's application records and verified by data from rain gages installed in fields.

[4]Precipitation measured at the Colorado Agricultural Meteorological Network Fort Morgan station.

[5]Crop evapotranspiration estimated by using the evapotranspiration calculator provided by the Colorado Agricultural Meteorological Network at http://ccc.atmos.colostate.edu/cgi-bin/extended_etr_form.pl. Crop evapotranspiration was calculated using the Penman-Monteith combination equation (Jensen and others, 1990) with data from the Colorado Agricultural Meteorological Network Fort Morgan station.

[6]Estimated recharge at sites L2 and L3 in 2008 is not reported because furrows overlying lysimeters were not used in 2008.

[7]Recharge estimated by water balance calculated as net irrigation plus precipitation minus consumptive use.

water at site L2 and 30 percent of applied water at site L3. Net irrigation of flood-irrigated fields (table 4) represents average uniform application across the field. Because flood-furrow irrigation may be nonuniform due to differences in soil permeability, irrigation exposure time, and location relative to the distribution system, net irrigation over lysimeters at flood-irrigated sites might not be representative of net irrigation at other locations within the field.

Precipitation measured at the Colorado Agricultural Meteorological Network (CoAgMet) Fort Morgan weather station (fig. 2) located about 8 mi west of Fort Morgan was used to represent precipitation at each site. Drainage measured by lysimeters was used as a direct estimate of recharge beneath irrigated fields. Recharge estimated by lysimeter drainage assumes evapotranspiration at the depth (4 ft) of lysimeter collector plates is negligible and that water percolating deeper than 4 ft ultimately reaches the water table. As indicated by the depth of chloride peaks in soil profiles beneath native and nonirrigated areas (see "Precipitation Infiltration"), some evapotranspiration may occur at depths greater than 4 ft, and lysimeter drainage may overestimate recharge.

Recharge estimated by lysimeter drainage (table 4) measured beneath irrigated fields varies by irrigation method, soil type, crop type, and the net quantity of irrigation water applied. Crop types at each site were selected by farmers each year as part of their normal operations. Recharge estimated by lysimeter drainage beneath the sprinkler-irrigated field on loam soil (site L1; alfalfa) ranged from 1.0 to 1.8 inches, which equals 5–7 percent of net irrigation (table 4) and 4–6 percent of net irrigation plus precipitation. The ratio of lysimeter drainage to net irrigation varies only slightly between 2007 and 2008, likely because the same crop was grown and irrigation conditions were similar in each year.

Recharge estimated by lysimeter drainage beneath the sprinkler-irrigated field on sandy soil (site L4; corn 2007, alfalfa 2008) ranged from 3.0 to 4.0 inches (table 4), which equals 23–30 percent of net irrigation and 17–26 percent of net irrigation plus precipitation. Lysimeter drainage in 2008 is more than in 2007, likely because the newly planted alfalfa crop in 2008 had less vegetative cover and consumptive use (table 4) than the corn crop in 2007, allowing more irrigation water to percolate below the root zone. The ratio of lysimeter drainage to net irrigation in both years at site L4 is more than at site L1, likely because the sandy soils at site L4 are more permeable than the loam soils at site L1, allowing more deep percolation to occur.

Recharge estimated by lysimeter drainage beneath flood-irrigated fields on loam soil at sites L2 (wheat 2007) and L3 (corn 2007) ranged from 0.1 to 3.5 inches (table 4), which equals 13–20 percent of net irrigation and 5–11 percent of net irrigation plus precipitation. Recharge at site L3 is larger than at site L2 because substantially more irrigation water was applied to the field at site L3 than at site L2. Variation in the ratio of lysimeter drainage to net irrigation at sites 2 and 3 likely is caused primarily by differences in soil

permeability and the extent to which assumed uniform net irrigation represents actual net irrigation over the lysimeter at each site. Lysimeter drainage measured at sites 2 and 3 in 2008 was not used to estimate recharge beneath flood-irrigated fields because furrows overlying the lysimeters were not used to irrigate crops in 2008. Because of the potential variability of actual net irrigation over the area of flood-irrigated fields, recharge estimates for flood-irrigated fields have larger uncertainty than recharge estimates for sprinkler-irrigated fields.

Water-Balance Method

Recharge beneath irrigated agricultural fields also was estimated for this study by using a water-balance method for comparison to recharge estimates based on lysimeter drainage. The control volume for recharge estimated by the water-balance method at each site is a soil column of unit surface area extending from land surface to the depth of effective evapotranspiration. Recharge estimated by the water-balance method for each period of measurement (table 4) was calculated as:

$$R = I_{net} + P - E_t + \Delta S \qquad (5)$$

where

R is recharge, in inches;

I_{net} is net irrigation water applied (total application minus estimated runoff), in inches;

P is precipitation, in inches;

E_t is crop evapotranspiration (consumptive use), in inches;

and

ΔS is net change in soil water stored in the unsaturated zone, in inches.

Each component of equation 5 was calculated as the sum of all daily values in each measurement period. Net irrigation and precipitation values used to estimate recharge by the water-balance method (table 4) were the same as those used to estimate the ratio of lysimeter drainage to net irrigation and net irrigation plus precipitation. Net change in soil moisture stored in the unsaturated zone is assumed equal to zero because each measurement period generally extends 15 days beyond the last irrigation event and allows sufficient time for transient increases in soil moisture resulting from irrigation to subside. The assumption that soil-moisture changes in the unsaturated zone are negligible over sufficiently long periods is supported by Susong (1995), who measured soil moisture throughout the irrigation season at flood- and sprinkler-irrigated sites having similar climatic and soil conditions to those in this study. Susong (1995) concluded that soil-moisture changes caused by irrigation were transient (lasting a few days), and soil moisture did not change substantially in the unsaturated zone between the beginning and end of the irrigation season. Crop evapotranspiration (consumptive use) was estimated for the period of lysimeter measurements at each site by using the evapotranspiration calculator provided by CoAgMet at *http://ccc.atmos.colostate.edu/cgi-bin/extended_etr_form.pl*, which can compute daily evapotranspiration using the Penman-Monteith combination equation as presented by Jensen and others (1990) (Troy Bauder, Colorado State University, written commun., 2008). A general form of the Penman-Monteith combination equation (Jensen and others, 1990) can be written as:

$$\lambda E = \frac{\Delta(R_n - G) + \rho c_p (e_z^o - e_z)/r_a}{\Delta + \gamma^*} \quad (6)$$

where

λE is latent heat flux density, in megajoules per square meter per day;

Δ is slope of saturation vapor-pressure temperature curve, in kilopascals per degree Celsius;

R_n is net radiation, in megajoules per square meter per day;

G is heat-flux density to the ground, megajoules per square meter per day;

ρ is air density, in kilograms per cubic meter;

c_p *is* specific heat of air at constant pressure, in megajoules per kilogram per degree Celsius;

e_z^o is saturation vapor pressure of air at height z above evapotranspiration surface, in kilopascals;

e_z is actual vapor pressure of air at height z above evapotranspiration surface, in kilopascals;

r_a is aerodynamic resistance to sensible heat and vapor transfer, calculated as

$$\frac{ln[(z_w - d)/z_{om}]ln[(z_p - d)/z_{ov}]}{(0.41)^2 u_z},$$

γ^* is calculated $\gamma(1 + r_c/r_a)$,

z_w is height of windspeed measurement, in meters;

d is displacement height of crop, in meters;

z_{om} is roughness length for momentum transfer, in meters;

z_p is height of humidity and temperature measurements, in meters;

z_{ov} is roughness length for vapor transfer, in meters;

u_z is windspeed at height z_w, in meters per second;

γ is psychometric constant, in kilopascals per degree Celsius;

and

r_c is crop canopy resistance, in seconds per meter.

Meteorological data required for computing daily evapotranspiration were obtained from the CoAgMet Fort Morgan station located about 8 mi west of the city of Fort Morgan. Total crop evapotranspiration was estimated by summing daily evapotranspiration during the period of analysis. Planting and harvest dates were provided by the farmer at each site. Alfalfa crops at site L1 and L4 were cut multiple times during the period of analysis, and alfalfa crops were assumed to become

reestablished (green up) 5 days after each cut for the purpose of estimating evapotranspiration. The accuracy of recharge estimates calculated by using the water-balance method can vary, depending on a number of factors. Because recharge estimated by the water-balance method is calculated as the residual of all other components of equation 5, the accuracy of the estimates depends on the accuracy with which the other components are estimated. Because the magnitude of recharge is smaller than that of the other variables, small changes in values of those variables can result in relatively large changes in recharge estimates. Recharge estimated by the water-balance method also can be sensitive to the period of time over which estimates are made. Over the period of measurement, cumulative crop evapotranspiration can exceed the sum of net irrigation and precipitation, and estimated recharge will be zero. Recharge may be occurring during short-term events, such as when irrigation water is applied, but the longer-term water balance does not consider these events.

Recharge estimated for this study by the water-balance method (table 4) has a wider range of values than recharge estimated by lysimeter drainage, likely because recharge estimated by the water-balance method is sensitive to inaccuracies in the estimates of other water-balance components. Recharge estimated by the water-balance method at site L1 (sprinkler-irrigated field on loam soil) ranges from 0.0 to 5.0 inches, which equals 0–19 percent of net irrigation and 0–16 percent of net irrigation plus precipitation.

Recharge estimated by the water-balance method at site L4 (sprinkler-irrigated field on sandy soil) is zero in both 2007 and 2008 (table 4) because cumulative evapotranspiration exceeded cumulative net irrigation plus precipitation over the period of measurement in each year. The water-balance method likely underestimates recharge at site L4 because the highly permeable soils at the site may allow water to percolate rapidly below the root zone before full potential evapotranspiration can occur at the time scale measured.

Recharge estimated by the water-balance method at sites L2 and L3 (flood-irrigated fields on loam soil) ranges from 0.0 to 11.3 inches (table 4), which equals 0–43 percent of net irrigation and 0–37 percent of net irrigation plus precipitation. Although the average ratio of recharge to net irrigation based on the water-balance method (22 percent) for the two sites is similar to that based on lysimeter drainage (17 percent), the range of values estimated by the water-balance method is much larger, and the ratio of recharge to net irrigation determined for each site individually is substantially different using the two methods.

Ditch and Reservoir Seepage

Seepage beneath irrigation ditches in the Lost Creek basin varies depending on such factors as ditch construction, ditch water stage, and soil permeability. Lowline Canal (fig. 4) and the portion of Prospect Lateral Ditch between Prospect Reservoir and Highway 79 are unlined; all other laterals and sublaterals in the Henrylyn Irrigation District that deliver water to the Lost Creek basin have been lined with cement since the 1980s (Rodney Baumgartner, Henrylyn Irrigation District, oral commun., 2008). Total water loss (including evaporation) along the unlined ditches varies over the irrigation season and is estimated to range from about 10 to 50 percent, depending on the water stage in the ditches (Rodney Baumgartner, Henrylyn Irrigation District, oral commun., 2008). Code (1945) estimated seepage loss from ditches delivering water to the Lost Creek basin to be about 33 percent. Assuming a seepage loss of 30 percent, about 1,290 of the average 4,300 acre-ft released by Prospect Reservoir during 1990–2001 would be lost to seepage along the Prospect Lateral Ditch and about 840 of the average 2,800 acre-ft diverted into Lowline Canal would be lost to seepage. Seepage losses from ditches lined with cement likely are substantially less than losses from unlined ditches, but the percentage of water lost is not known.

Water delivered to Olds Reservoir is used primarily to recharge the alluvial aquifer of the Lost Creek basin. Seepage beneath Olds Reservoir has been estimated by several studies (Code, 1945; Glover, 1959; Skinner, 1963) to range from about 17 to 70 acre-ft/d with most variation caused by differences in reservoir stage. Based on a reservoir surface area of about 58 acres (Skinner, 1963), the average seepage rate estimated by these studies ranged from about 0.3 to 1.2 ft/d over the area of the reservoir when the reservoir contained water.

Delivery records provided for this study by the Henrylyn Irrigation District (Rodney Baumgartner, written commun., 2008) indicate an average of 2,955 acre-ft (table 5) of water was delivered annually to Olds Reservoir over an average of 70 days during each year from 1990 to 2001. Because most water delivered to Olds Reservoir is during the cool nonirrigation season and seepage from the reservoir is rapid, evaporative losses are small and nearly all water delivered to Olds Reservoir likely recharges the Lost Creek basin. Assuming all water delivered to Olds Reservoir becomes recharge, the average seepage rate from the reservoir on an annual basis (including days that water was not in the reservoir) during 1990–2001 was about 8 acre-ft/d (0.14 ft/d over the reservoir's surface area).

Seepage beneath Lord Reservoir was estimated by Code (1945) to be about 8 acre-ft/d at very low stage and by Skinner (1963) to be about 25 acre-ft/d at full stage. Based on a reservoir surface area of about 170 acres (Schupbach and Lewis, 1996a), the average seepage rate over the area of the reservoir at very low stage was then 0.05 ft/d, and the average seepage rate over the reservoir's area at full stage was 0.15 ft/d.

During 1990–92 (no data were available for 1993–2001), water was stored in Lord Reservoir an average of 54 days (Colorado Division of Water Resources, 2008). Assuming the average seepage rate from Lord Reservoir is 17 acre-ft/d (mean seepage rate of very low stage and full stage), average annual seepage from Lord Reservoir during 1990–92 was about 918 acre-ft, and the average seepage rate from the reservoir on an annual basis (including days water was not stored in the reservoir) during 1990–92 was 2.5 acre-ft/d (0.015 ft/d over the reservoir's surface area).

Table 5. Annual water deliveries to Olds Reservoir for recharge to the Lost Creek Designated Ground Water Basin.

[acre-ft, acre-feet; acre-ft/d, acre-ft per day; ft/d, feet per day; –, infrequent diversion records]

Year	Total water delivered for recharge[1] (acre-ft)	Number of days water delivered[2]	Annually averaged seepage rate[3] (acre-ft/d)	Annually averaged seepage rate over reservoir area[4] (ft/d)
1990	2,041	39	6	0.10
1991	2,758	69	8	0.13
1992	2,362	99	6	0.11
1993	3,280	–	9	0.15
1994	2,792	84	8	0.13
1995	5,258	104	14	0.25
1996	1,726	48	5	0.08
1997	1,660	42	5	0.08
1998	2,769	64	8	0.13
1999	2,805	55	8	0.13
2000	2,528	50	7	0.12
2001	5,480	117	15	0.26
Average	2,955	70	8	0.14

[1]Total water delivered for recharge provided by Rodney Baumgartner, Henrylyn Irrigation District, written commun., 2008.

[2]Number of days water delivered from Colorado Division of Water Resources (2008).

[3]Annually averaged seepage rate calculated as total water delivered for recharge divided by 365 days per year.

[4]Annually averaged seepage rate over reservoir area calculated as annually averaged seepage rate divided by a reservoir surface area of 58 acres.

Seepage beneath Prospect Reservoir has not been estimated but likely is small because the reservoir is located near the western margin of the Lost Creek basin, where the alluvial aquifer is thin or absent. Based on geologic mapping by Bryant and others (1981) (fig. 5) and aquifer mapping presented by Schupbach and Lewis (1995), much of Prospect Reservoir appears to be directly underlain by bedrock strata of the Arapahoe aquifer rather than alluvial sediments. Therefore seepage into the Lost Creek basin from Prospect Reservoir likely occurs only along the east side of the reservoir, where the reservoir contacts the alluvial aquifer of the Lost Creek basin.

Subsurface Inflow

Although the alluvial aquifer of the Lost Creek basin is bounded by bedrock along most of its eastern, western, and southern edges, the main part of the aquifer (primarily in the main paleovalley) may receive subsurface inflow from upgradient tributary valleys that are within the basin's administrative extent. The main part of the aquifer also may receive irrigation return flow from ditch seepage and deep percolation of water beneath irrigated fields that are located upgradient and west of the main aquifer but are within the basin's administrative extent. Because data concerning inflow from tributary valleys and irrigation return flow are lacking, flows from these sources are unknown but likely are relatively small in comparison to other sources of recharge to the basin.

Discharge

Discharge from the Lost Creek basin occurs primarily as well withdrawals, evapotranspiration, and outflow to the South Platte River valley at the north end of the basin. Depending on the hydraulic gradient between the alluvial aquifer of the Lost Creek basin and the underlying Denver Basin bedrock aquifers, discharge also can occur to the bedrock aquifers, but because the hydraulic conductivity of the bedrock aquifers is much smaller than that of the alluvial aquifer, discharge to the bedrock aquifers likely is small compared to recharge from other sources. Estimation of discharge to the bedrock aquifers from the Lost Creek basin is beyond the scope of this report.

Well Withdrawals

Groundwater withdrawals in the Lost Creek basin are primarily from high-capacity irrigation wells. Groundwater also is withdrawn from small-capacity wells, such as domestic and stock wells, and a small number of municipal wells, but total withdrawals from these wells are estimated to be small compared to withdrawals from irrigation wells. About 266 decreed irrigation wells (fig. 16) are located in the Lost Creek basin with final permits (finalized water rights) on file with the CDWR (Suzanne Sellers, Colorado Division of Water Resources, written commun., 2007). Most wells are located along the main paleovalley in the central and northern parts of the basin where the saturated thickness of the aquifer is greatest. Average annual historical withdrawals previously were estimated for 39 irrigation wells in the Lost Creek basin as part of a legal stipulation concerning a change in water use for the wells (William Fronczac, Gateway American Resources, written commun., 2005). Average annual historical withdrawals generally were estimated for the stipulation based on power-conversion coefficients and power-use records from 1985 to 1994 if power-use records were available for those years and from 1982 to 1985 if power-use records were not available for 1985–94. During 1990–94 (the period included in this study) average annual withdrawals from the 34 wells for which data were available during this time period were estimated by the stipulation to range from about 38.8 to 353.0 acre-ft per well (Appendix 5) with an average value of 157.2 acre-ft per well. Average annual withdrawals per unit area of land irrigated by each well ranged from about 0.9 to 2.4 acre-ft/acre with an average value of about 1.6 acre-ft/acre.

Average annual withdrawals from irrigation wells lacking power-use data are assumed similar to withdrawals by wells with power-use data. Average annual withdrawals from wells lacking power-use data were estimated for this study by multiplying the average annual withdrawal per unit area (1.6 acre-ft/acre) of all wells with power-use data by the number of estimated acres irrigated by each well lacking power-use data. The number of acres irrigated by an individual well in a group of commingled wells was estimated by apportioning the total number of commingled acres by the number of acres permitted for each individual well. Average annual withdrawals from irrigation wells lacking power-use data are estimated to range from about 32 to

581 acre-ft with an average value of 168 acre-ft (Appendix 5). Assuming all decreed irrigation wells (with and without power-use data) with final permits in the Lost Creek basin were actively used during 1990–2001, total average annual withdrawals from the wells are estimated to be about 44,300 acre-ft to irrigate about 27,800 acres.

Evapotranspiration

Water can be removed directly from the aquifer by the process of evapotranspiration in locations where the water table is shallower than the effective depth of evapotranspiration, and the rate of water removal by evapotranspiration generally increases as water-table depth decreases. In the Lost Creek basin, the water table generally is deeper than the effective depth of evapotranspiration. However, in the northern part of the basin, particularly in topographically low areas along drainages, the water table is shallow, and water likely is removed directly from the aquifer by evapotranspiration in at least some of these areas. Potential average annual evapotranspiration by grasses and shrubs in semiarid to arid areas has been estimated (Thorn, 1995; DeMeo and others, 2008) to range from about 23 to 34 inches. Evapotranspiration also can occur directly from the aquifer by phreatophytes (plants or trees with roots deep enough to reach the water table and take up water directly from the aquifer). Phreatophytes in the Lost Creek basin consist primarily of cottonwood trees growing near reservoirs and along drainages. Cottonwood roots have been estimated to extend up to 30 ft below land surface (Robinson, 1958), and average annual evapotranspiration by cottonwoods at 100-percent tree density has been estimated to range from about 62 to 97 inches where the water table is 3–4 ft below land surface. Evapotranspiration by grasses, shrubs, and cottonwoods in the Lost Creek basin is estimated to fall within the ranges estimated by Thorn (1995), DeMeo and others (2008), and Robinson (1958) based on similarity of climatic and hydrologic conditions.

Subsurface Outflow

Subsurface outflow at the north end of the Lost Creek basin to the South Platte River valley can be estimated using a form of Darcy's law (Fetter, 1994):

$$Q = -KA\,(dh/dl) \qquad (7)$$

where

Q is subsurface outflow, in cubic feet per day,
K is aquifer hydraulic conductivity, in feet per day,
A is aquifer cross-sectional area, in square feet,

and

dh/dl is water-table hydraulic gradient (dimensionless).

The negative sign on the right side of equation 7 is used to denote the direction of groundwater flow, which in this instance is out of the aquifer. Using representative values of hydraulic conductivity (150 ft/d; table 2), cross-sectional area (1,000,000 ft²), and water-table hydraulic gradient (0.005) (Nelson, Haley,

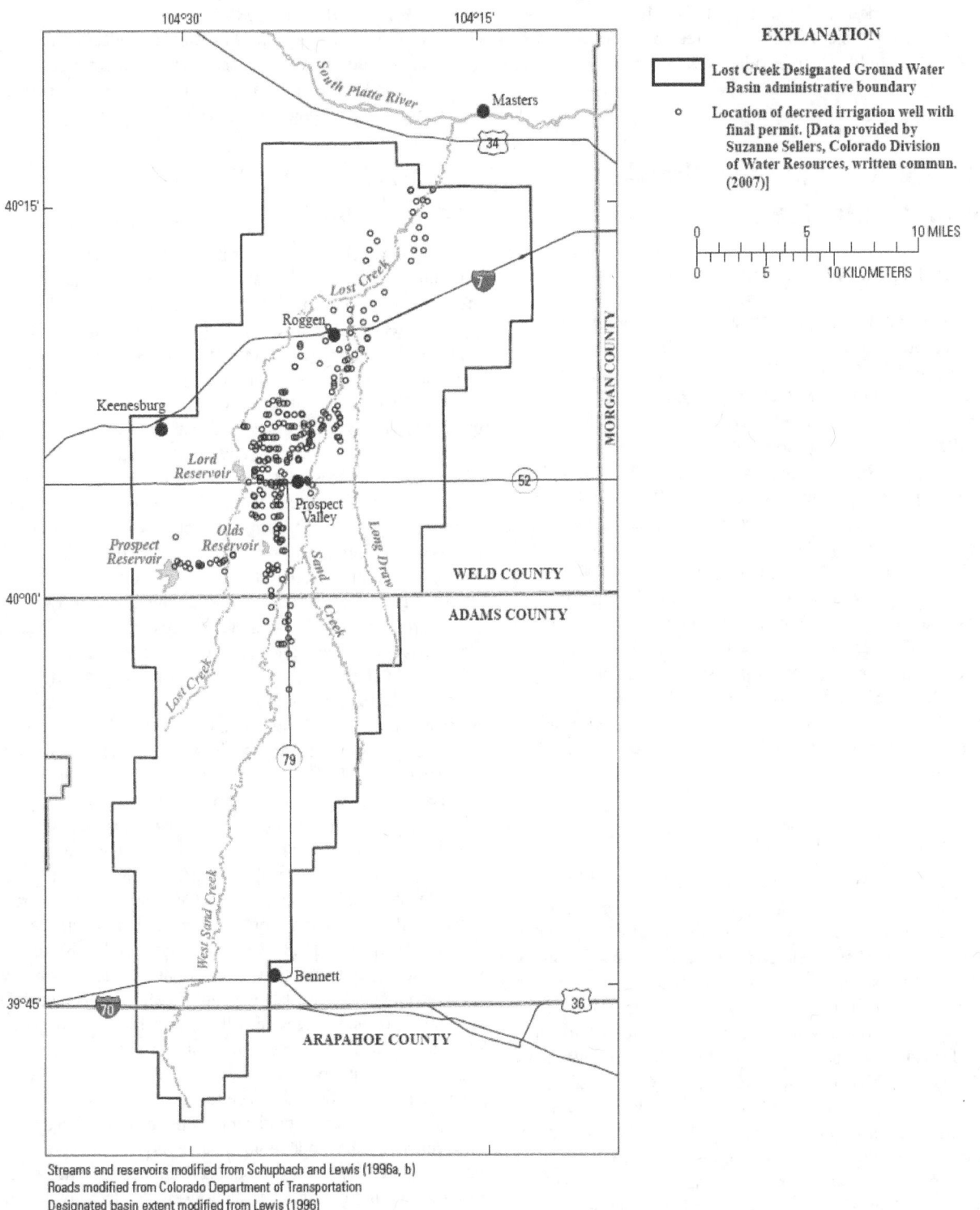

Streams and reservoirs modified from Schupbach and Lewis (1996a, b)
Roads modified from Colorado Department of Transportation
Designated basin extent modified from Lewis (1996)
North American Datum of 1983

Figure 16.   Location of decreed irrigation wells with final permits in the Lost Creek Designated Ground Water Basin, Colorado.

Patterson, and Quirk, Inc., 1967, plate 3) of the Lost Creek alluvial aquifer at the north end of the Lost Creek basin, subsurface outflow to the South Platte River valley, calculated using equation 7, is 750,000 ft³/d (17.2 acre-ft/d).

Steady-State Numerical Simulation of Groundwater Flow

Previous Groundwater Flow Model

In 1995, Hatton Water Consultants, Inc., constructed a numerical groundwater flow model of part of the Lost Creek basin using the U.S. Geological Survey finite-difference computer code MODFLOW–88 (McDonald and Harbaugh, 1988) to quantitatively evaluate the effects of a proposed well field under different pumping and artificial-recharge scenarios (Thomas Hatton, JR Engineering, written commun., 2004). The model subsequently was modified between 1995 and 2004 and used to predict the effects of additional pumping scenarios under different recharge and hydrogeologic conditions (Barbara Ford, HRS Water Consultants, Inc., written commun., 2005). Formal documentation does not accompany the modified model versions (Barbara Ford, HRS Water Consultants, Inc., written commun., 2005). Description of the 2004 version of the groundwater flow model presented below is based on examination of the MODFLOW–88 input files and information provided by Thomas Hatton (JR Engineering, written commun., 2004) and Barbara Ford (HRS Water Consultants, Inc., oral commun., 2004; written commun., 2005).

Design of Previous Model

The 2004 version of the model simulated steady-state groundwater flow in the Lost Creek basin using one layer and unconfined conditions. The model was calibrated to 24 hydraulic-head observations representing average water-table conditions in the Lost Creek basin. Dates of hydraulic-head observations were not provided. The model was not calibrated to flow observations representing groundwater discharge to streams because no perennial streams exist in the basin. The model grid has 89 rows and 53 columns with a maximum cell size of 2,640 ft × 2,640 ft and grid refinement to 782 ft × 782 ft near wells and reservoirs. The eastern, southern, and western model edges were simulated as no-flow boundaries near the limit of zero saturated thickness indicated by Nelson, Haley, Patterson, and Quirk, Inc. (1967). The northern model edge was simulated as a constant-head boundary aligned east to west across the basin. The model base was simulated as a no-flow boundary with a configuration based on the altitude of the bedrock surface mapped by Nelson, Haley, Patterson, and Quirk, Inc. (1967), and subsequent borehole exploration (Barbara Ford, HRS Water Consultants, Inc., oral commun., 2004). The upper model boundary is defined by the water table. Initial hydraulic-conductivity values were estimated from aquifer-test results reported by Nelson, Haley, Patterson,

and Quirk, Inc. (1967), and HRS Water Consultants, Inc. (written commun., 2006), and adjusted based on model calibration. Hydraulic-conductivity values used in the model ranged from 45 to 360 ft/d with values generally being greatest near the center of the basin and decreasing toward the basin margins.

Inflows and Outflows Simulated by Previous Model

Aquifer recharge was distributed on the basis of model calibration and limited available data. Recharge values used in the model ranged from 0 in/yr for an area assumed to discharge groundwater near the northern model boundary to 43.8 in/yr beneath part of Prospect Reservoir and for a small area along the west model boundary in the northern part of the basin. Recharge in the northern part of the basin was simulated as 3.7 in/yr where groundwater was not assumed to discharge. Recharge in the middle part of the basin generally ranged from about 1.5–2.6 in/yr with the lower values near the center of the basin, away from basin margins. Recharge in the southern part of the basin was about 1.9 in/yr. Seepage from Prospect Reservoir and Lord Reservoir was simulated by using zones of greater recharge with values ranging from about 11.0 to 43.8 in/yr at reservoir locations. Zones of greater recharge were added downgradient from reservoirs during model calibration. Recharge occurring from seepage along irrigation ditches and ephemeral stream channels was considered in total estimated recharge but was not explicitly specified at ditch and stream locations. Inflow from the underlying Denver Basin aquifers was not simulated. Olds Reservoir was simulated as an area of specified inflow to the aquifer by using the Well package of MODFLOW. The simulated rate of inflow from Olds Reservoir was about 2.74 acre-ft/d (1,000 acre-ft/yr).

Well pumping was simulated as net withdrawals from an individual well or all wells within a cell, based on the amount of water consumed as a result of irrigation. Therefore, net well withdrawals reflected total estimated pumping minus return flow to the aquifer from infiltration of water applied to fields. An average net withdrawal of 1.23 acre-ft/acre was used for simulated wells unless specific withdrawal information was available. Wells for which net withdrawals were known were assigned actual net withdrawal rates, whereas net withdrawals for other irrigation wells in the Lost Creek basin were estimated by multiplying the average net withdrawal rate by the number of acres irrigated by each well or all wells within a cell.

The maximum evapotranspiration rate was defined as uniform across the model domain at 35 in/yr, but evapotranspiration occurred at only a few model cells in the northern part of the basin where the water table is shallow enough to be within the specified extinction depth of 10 ft.

Updated Groundwater Flow Model

An updated numerical groundwater flow model of the Lost Creek basin was constructed using information from previous investigations and data collected and compiled by this study. The USGS modular groundwater modeling program,

MODFLOW–2000 (Harbaugh and others, 2000) was used to simulate steady-state groundwater flow in the updated model. The preconditioned conjugate-gradient 2 (PCG2) solver (Hill, 1990) was used to solve the groundwater-flow equations produced by MODFLOW-2000. Pre- and postprocessing of MODFLOW–2000 files primarily were completed using the MODFLOW Graphical User Interface (Winston, 2000) for the Argus ONE geographic information system (Argus Interware, 1997). The model was calibrated by using the Observation, Sensitivity, and Parameter-Estimation Processes (Hill and others, 2000) of MODFLOW–2000.

Design of Updated Model

The alluvial aquifer of the Lost Creek basin is represented by using a 1-layer model grid (fig. 17) with 191 rows and 70 columns having uniform cell dimensions of 1,000 ft × 1,000 ft. The model simulates groundwater flow under unconfined conditions with the rewetting capability active. The spatial extent of active model cells generally is limited to areas where saturated thickness is greater than 10 ft. The area of Hay Gulch (fig. 6), in the northeastern part of the Lost Creek basin, is not included in the active model extent because relatively shallow bedrock appears to separate Hay Gulch from the main paleovalley of the Lost Creek basin, and saturated thickness in the area between Hay Gulch and the main paleovalley generally appears to be less than about 10 ft except within 1–2 mi of the northern boundary of the Lost Creek basin, where saturated thickness is estimated to be about 20 ft (Nelson, Haley, Patterson, and Quirk, Inc.,1967, pl. 3). Model layer thickness varies from about 10 to 190 ft as determined by the thickness of regolith sediments mapped as part of this study (see "Aquifer Extent and Thickness"). The top of the model is defined as the altitude of the land surface derived from the USGS National Elevation Data Set (NED) with 10-m resolution (U.S. Geological Survey, 2002). The model base is defined as the altitude of the land surface minus regolith thickness.

Four zones (fig. 18) are used to represent the spatial distribution of horizontal hydraulic conductivity in the model. The hydraulic-conductivity distribution estimated from aquifer and specific-capacity tests (fig. 11) was used to define initial (precalibrated) hydraulic conductivity within the model, and the distribution of hydraulic conductivity was adjusted during model calibration. Hydraulic conductivity of zones 1, 2, 3, and 4 are represented by parameters HK_1, HK_2, HK_3, and HK_4, respectively.

Boundary Conditions and Hydrologic Stresses

The base of the model is simulated as a no-flow boundary to represent relatively low permeability bedrock in contact with the alluvial aquifer. The eastern, western, and southern edges of the model also are simulated as no-flow boundaries (fig. 17) except in small areas where general-head boundaries are simulated by using the General-Head Boundary Package of MODFLOW–2000. General-head boundaries allow groundwater to flow into or out of the model in proportion to the difference between hydraulic head at the boundary and a user-specified hydraulic head external to the model (McDonald and Harbaugh, 1988). Simulated hydraulic head also can vary at the boundary. The northern (downgradient) edge of the model is simulated as a general-head boundary to allow groundwater flow and hydraulic head at the boundary to change in response to simulated hydrologic stresses. Hydraulic conductance of the general-head boundary at the downgradient edge of the model is represented by the parameter GHB_Out. General-head boundaries along parts of the eastern, western, and southern edges of the model simulate inflow from tributary valleys at the edge of the model domain and irrigation return flow from ditch seepage and deep percolation of water beneath irrigated fields located upgradient and west of the model domain (fig. 17). Hydraulic conductances of the general-head boundaries used to simulate inflow from tributary valleys and from irrigation return flow along the west model boundary are represented by the parameters GHB_In and GHB_Return, respectively. All general-head boundaries in the model are defined using a saturated thickness, hydraulic conductivity, and hydraulic gradient representative of the aquifer at each boundary location.

Areal recharge is simulated by using the Recharge Package of MODFLOW–2000 and is distributed by land use (fig. 19) and soil type. Recharge in nonirrigated areas (native grassland and nonirrigated agricultural fields) (parameter RCH_Nonirr) includes contributions from precipitation, stream-channel infiltration, and any other localized sources of recharge such as seepage from domestic septic systems, within the nonirrigated area. Recharge from infiltration of water in ephemeral stream channels is not explicitly simulated at the locations of stream channels in the model because stream channels are narrow compared to model cell size and are distributed relatively evenly throughout the southern part of the basin (fig. 1), where nonirrigated land is prevalent (fig. 4). Recharge from deep percolation of water beneath areas of irrigated agriculture is assigned on the basis of irrigation method (flood or sprinkler) and the distribution of irrigated acres in 2001, as mapped by Riverside Technology, Inc. (2007). About 28,000 (86.2 percent) of the 32,500 acres that are irrigated in the Lost Creek basin are within the domain of the simulated aquifer. Recharge beneath flood-irrigated fields is represented by the parameter RCH_Flood; recharge beneath sprinkler-irrigated fields is represented by the parameter RCH_Sprink. Because the location of ditches (Prospect Lateral Ditch, Lowline Canal, and the 1053 ditch) within the model domain generally coincides with the location of irrigated fields, and because ditches are narrow compared to model cell size, seepage from irrigation ditches within the model domain is not explicitly simulated by the model. Instead, seepage from ditches within the model domain is implicitly included as part of recharge occurring from deep percolation of water beneath irrigated fields. Recharge rates for all land uses are multiplied by 1.5 where sandy soils are present at the land surface to represent larger recharge rates in areas of sandy soil (fig. 20).

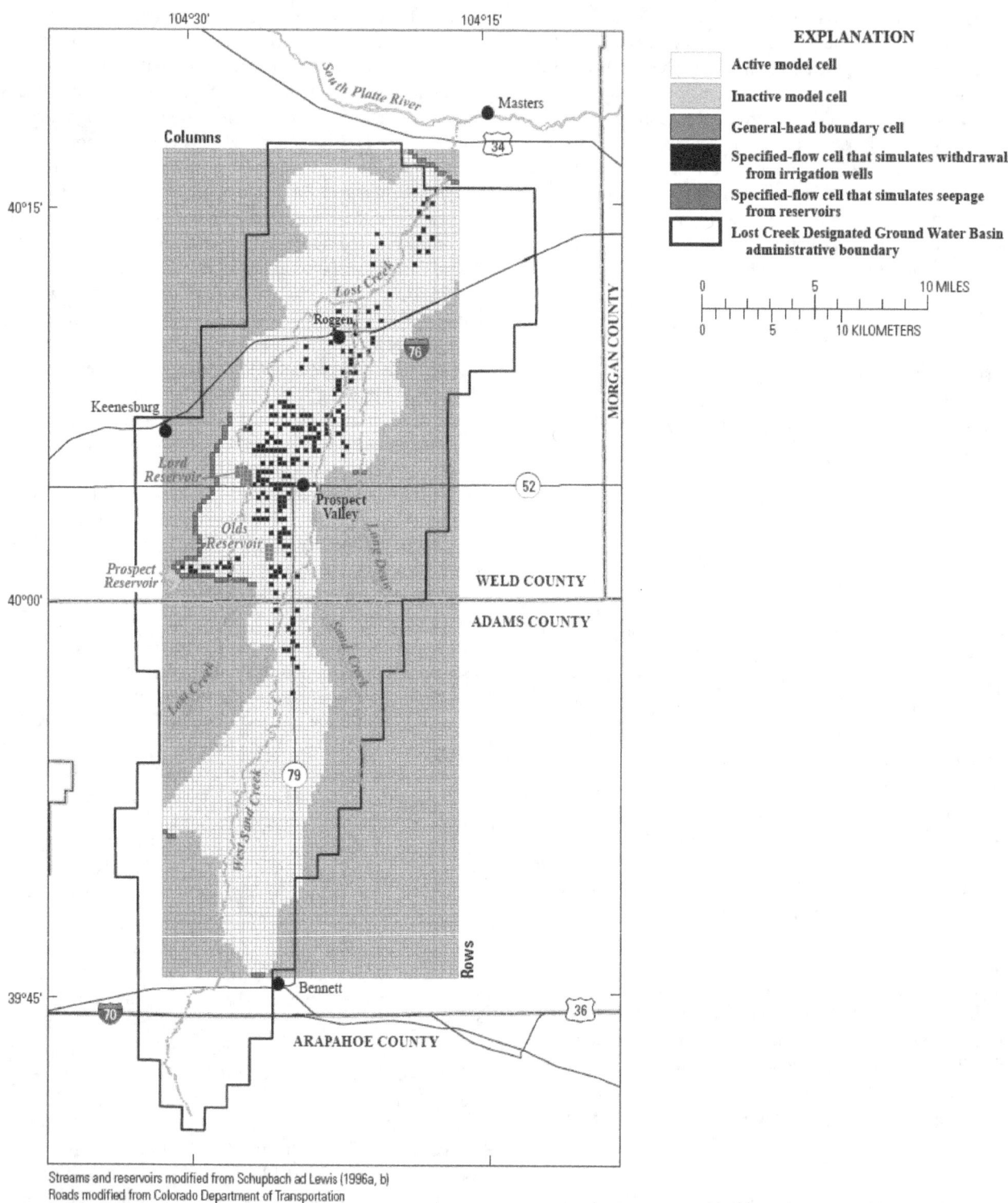

Streams and reservoirs modified from Schupbach ad Lewis (1996a, b)
Roads modified from Colorado Department of Transportation
Designated basin extent modified from Lewis (1996)
North American Datum of 1983

Figure 17.   Grid and boundary conditions of the groundwater flow model, Lost Creek Designated Ground Water Basin, Colorado.

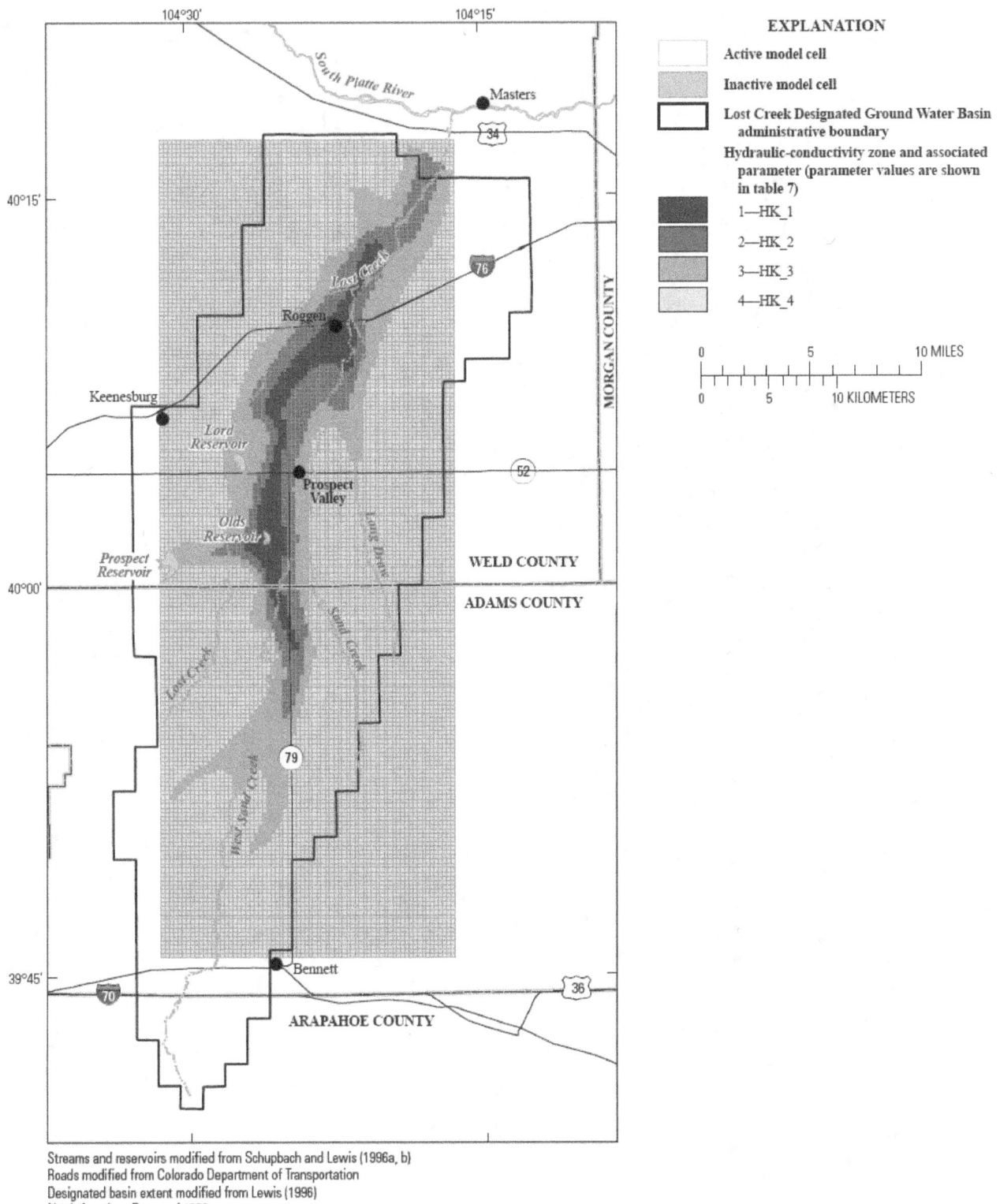

Figure 18.   Hydraulic conductivity zones of the groundwater flow model, Lost Creek Designated Ground Water Basin, Colorado.

Streams and reservoirs modified from Schupbach and Lewis (1996a, b)
Roads modified from Colorado Department of Transportation
Designated basin extent modified from Lewis (1996)
North American Datum of 1983

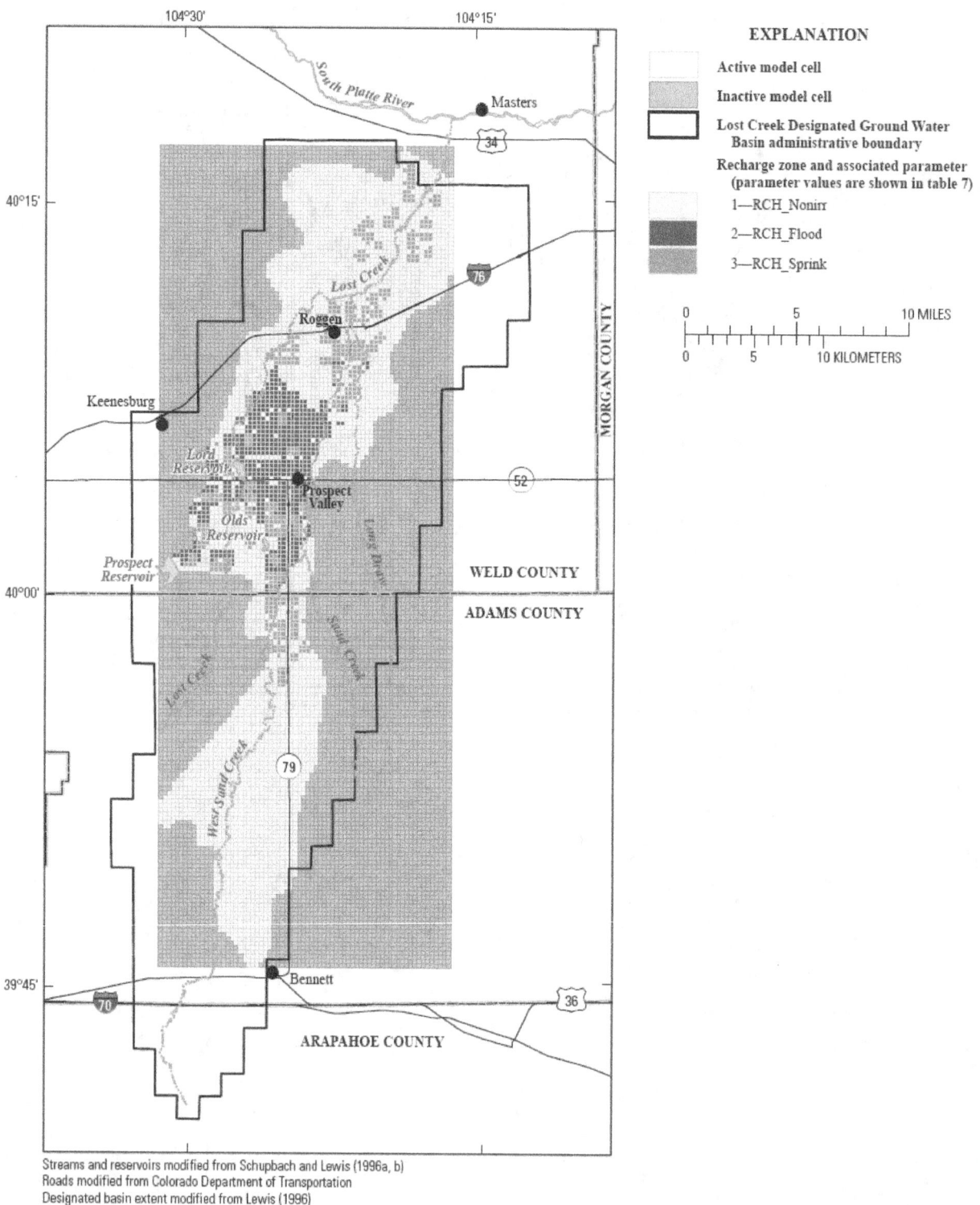

Streams and reservoirs modified from Schupbach and Lewis (1996a, b)
Roads modified from Colorado Department of Transportation
Designated basin extent modified from Lewis (1996)
North American Datum of 1983

Figure 19.   Recharge zones of the groundwater flow model, Lost Creek Designated Ground Water Basin, Colorado.

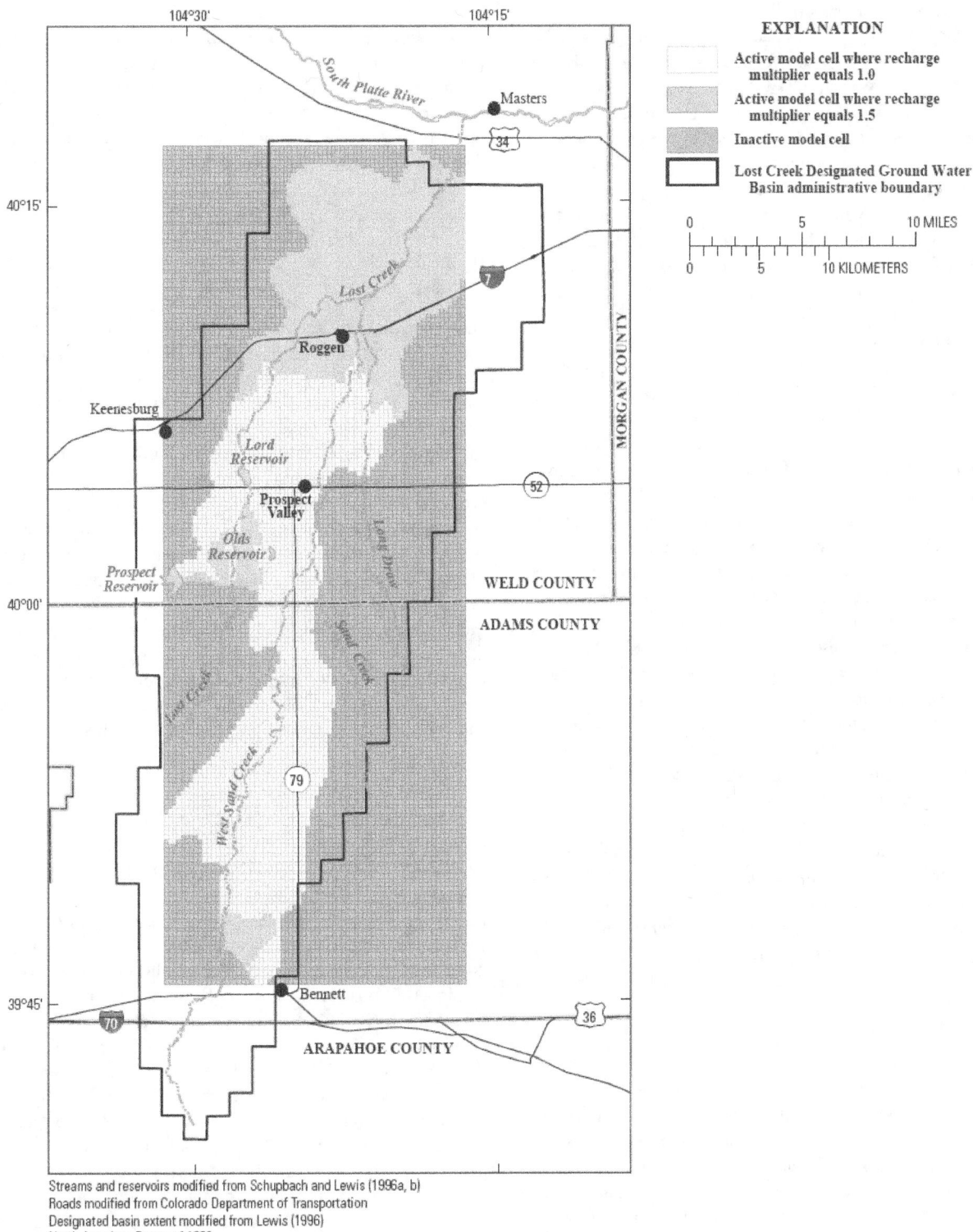

Figure 20. Multiplier array used to increase recharge in areas representing sandy soils in the groundwater flow model, Lost Creek Designated Ground Water Basin, Colorado.

Groundwater withdrawals from wells in the Lost Creek basin are simulated by using the Well Package of MODFLOW–2000. Withdrawals are simulated only for decreed irrigation wells with final permits on file with the CDWR. The average withdrawal rate per acre of irrigated land for wells with power-use (power-conversion coefficient) data is represented by the parameter Wells_PCC. The average withdrawal rate per acre of irrigated land for wells lacking power-use data is represented by the parameter Wells_Irr. Multipliers are used to compute the total volumetric withdrawal rate for each well simulated by the model. Multipliers for wells with power-use data are assigned values that convert average withdrawal rates per acre to total volumetric withdrawal rates estimated from power-use records for each well. Multipliers for wells lacking power-use data are assigned values equal to the estimated number of acres irrigated by each well (Appendix 5) to compute total volumetric withdrawal rates.

Seepage from Olds and Lord Reservoirs also is simulated by using the Well Package of MODFLOW–2000. Seepage is simulated as specified inflow of water at the locations of each reservoir. The seepage rate per unit area of Olds Reservoir is represented by the parameter Q_Olds. The seepage rate per unit area of Lord Reservoir is represented by the parameter Q_Lord. The volumetric seepage rate for each model cell simulating seepage from the reservoirs is computed by multiplying the seepage rate per unit area by the reservoir's area within each model cell. Because Prospect Reservoir is located at the edge of the model domain and appears to mainly overlie bedrock, seepage from Prospect Reservoir is simulated only along the east side of the reservoir by using the General-Head Boundary Package of MODFLOW–2000. Hydraulic conductance of the general-head boundary used to simulate seepage from Prospect Reservoir is represented by the parameter GHB_Prspct.

Evapotranspiration is simulated by using the Evapotranspiration (EVT) Package of MODFLOW–2000. Evapotranspiration is simulated throughout the model domain with an extinction depth of 5 ft, relative to NED-derived land-surface altitude. The maximum evapotranspiration rate is represented by parameter EVT_Par.

Model Calibration

The model was calibrated by using the Observation, Sensitivity, and Parameter-Estimation Processes of MODFLOW-2000 (Hill and others, 2000), which uses inverse modeling methods to minimize the difference between measured values and model-simulated values. The model primarily is calibrated to average hydrologic conditions during the period 1990–2001 because groundwater levels in the Lost Creek basin generally were relatively stable during that period.

To evaluate the viability of alternative conceptual models, calibration began with a simple model and complexity was added incrementally, based on the contribution of the added complexity to improving statistical measures of model fit and related measures. The hydraulic-conductivity distribution and model extent also were adjusted to evaluate their effect on calibration. Incremental additions that improved model calibration included

(1) simulation of inflow from tributary valleys at the edge of the model domain, (2) simulation of irrigation return flow along part of the west model boundary, (3) use of separate parameters for flood- and sprinkler-irrigation recharge, (4) use of a multiplier to increase recharge where sandy soils are present in the Lost Creek basin, (5) use of separate parameters for wells with power-use data and wells lacking power-use data, (6) simulation of seepage from Olds, Lord, and Prospect Reservoirs, and (7) simulation of evapotranspiration.

Observations

An observation is a measurement of actual conditions, such as hydraulic head or flow, that can be compared to a model-calculated value. Forty-three hydraulic-head observations (fig. 21; table 6) distributed throughout Lost Creek basin were used to calibrate the model. Hydraulic-head observations consist primarily of water-level measurements made during the period 1990–2001. However, hydraulic-head observations made during other years were used to calibrate the model at locations (primarily in the southern part of the basin) where data were not available for 1990–2001. At locations where multiple water-level measurements were made during 1990–2001, the average of all measurements made during the period is used to represent hydraulic head. Using statistical methods described by Hill (1998, p. 45–49), the standard deviation of measurement error for hydraulic-head observations is estimated to be about 3 ft. Because perennial streams do not exist in the Lost Creek basin, the model is not calibrated to flow observations representing streamflow gains or losses.

Prior Information

Data (such as results of aquifer tests or deep-percolation studies) used to estimate a parameter value by using inverse modeling methods is called prior information. Use of prior information allows direct measurements of model input values to be included in the calibration regression (Hill, 1998). Prior information is used in the Lost Creek basin model to reduce parameter correlation (possibly caused by a lack of flow observations) and obtain a well-posed regression problem for estimation of many parameters. Prior information was used to constrain estimates of parameters HK_1, HK_2, HK_3, RCH_Nonirr, RCH_Flood, RCH_Sprink, Wells_PCC, Wells_Irr, and Q_Olds. Prior-information values were assigned on the basis of initial parameter estimates; however, prior-information values for RCH_Nonirr and Wells_Irr were adjusted during calibration to promote convergence of the solution to the finite-difference equations used by the model. Weights for prior-information values initially were assigned on the basis of the standard deviation of calculated or estimated prior-information measurement error as described by Hill (1998, p. 45–49). However, to constrain estimated parameters to values near those indicated by prior information, values for parameters HK_1, HK_2, RCH_Flood, and Wells_Irr were regularized by using prior-information weights that are smaller than indicated by the standard deviation of prior-information measurement error. Weights used for prior-information values are presented in table 7.

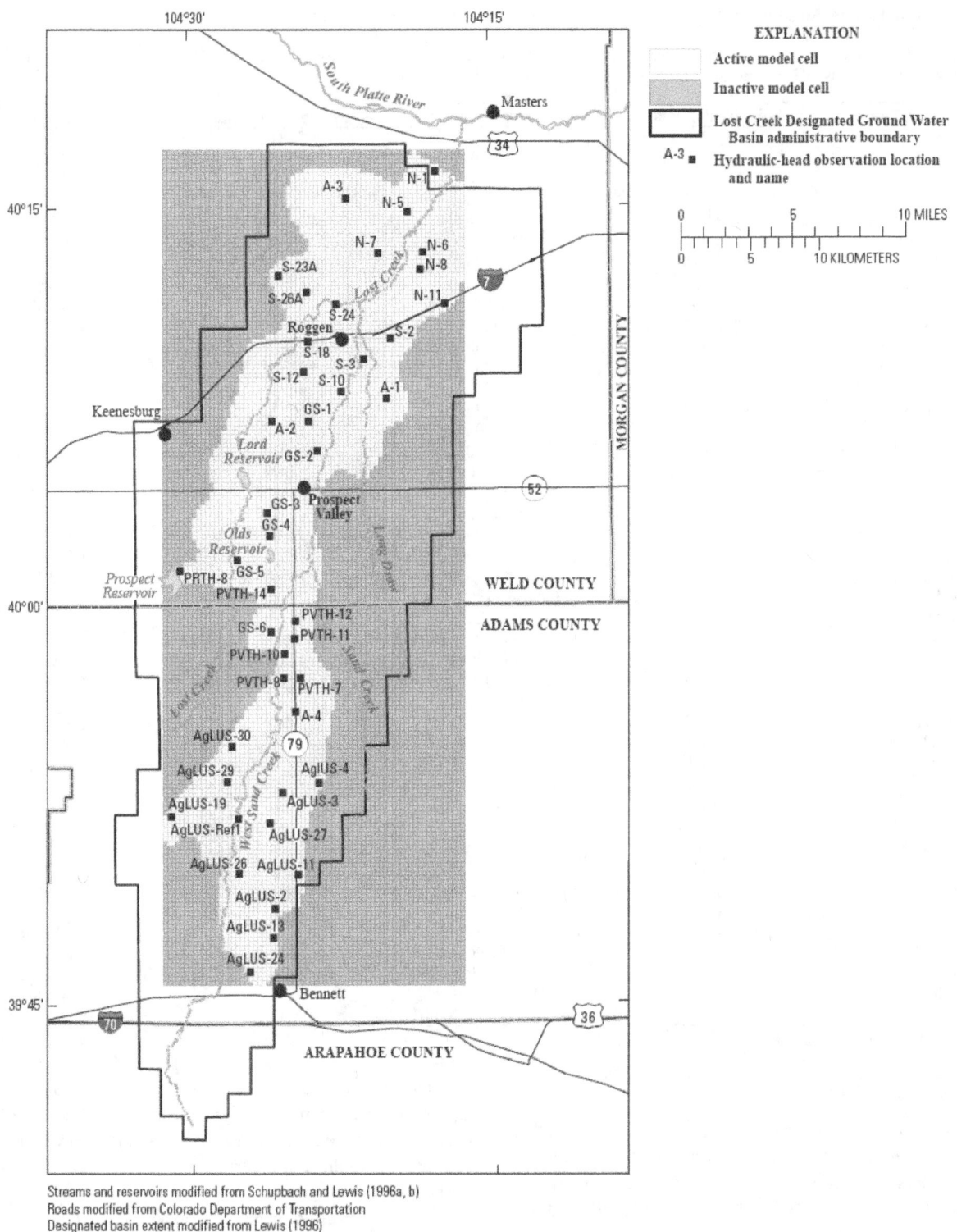

Figure 21.   Location of hydraulic-head observations used to calibrate the groundwater flow model, Lost Creek Designated Ground Water Basin, Colorado.

Table 6. Hydraulic-head observations used to calibrate the Lost Creek Designated Ground Water Basin model.

[Hydraulic head in feet above National Geodetic Vertical Datum of 1929; CDWR, Colorado Division of Water Resources; USGS, U.S. Geological Survey; HRS, HRS Water Consultants, Inc. (written commun., 2006); --, not known or not applicable]

Observation name	Hydraulic head[1]	Observation date(s)	Well permit number	Source
A-1	4,730	5/25/2002	57812-A	CDWR
A-2	4,747	5/10/2006	31555-FPR	CDWR
A-3	4,672	9/23/1981	121539-A	CDWR
A-4	4,977	3/13/1984	69045-A	CDWR
AgLUS-11	5,233	3/5/2003	MH-41855	USGS
AgLUS-13	5,342	3/10/2003	MH-41893	USGS
AgLUS-19	5,210	1/23/2003	MH-41723	USGS
AgLUS-2	5,304	3/6/2003	MH-41852	USGS
AgLUS-24	5,363	2/10/2003	MH-41720	USGS
AgLUS-26	5,245	1/20/2003	MH-41688	USGS
AgLUS-27	5,158	1/14/2003	MH-41652	USGS
AgLUS-29	5,109	2/6/2003	MH-41725	USGS
AgLUS-3	5,117	3/2/2003	MH-41856	USGS
AgLUS-30	5,074	1/13/2003	MH-41648	USGS
AgLUS-4	5,108	3/5/2003	MH-41853	USGS
AgLUS-REF1	5,172	2/7/2003	MH-41787	USGS
GS-1	4,742	1990–2001	--	CDWR
GS-2	4,758	1991–1999	--	CDWR
GS-3	4,825	1990–2001	--	CDWR
GS-4	4,838	1990–2001	6693-R	CDWR
GS-5	4,875	1990–2001	--	CDWR
GS-6	4,897	1990–2001	14856-R	CDWR
N-1	4,539	1990–93, 1995–2001	--	CDWR
N-11	4,682	1990–2001	--	CDWR
N-5	4,589	1991–93, 1995–2001	--	CDWR
N-6	4,609	1990–2001	12174-F	CDWR
N-7	4,632	1990–99	12225-F	CDWR
N-8	4,626	1991–2001	--	CDWR
PRTH-8	4,972	5/19/1999	--	HRS
PVTH-10	4,918	3/18/1997	--	HRS
PVTH-11	4,895	3/18/1997	--	HRS
PVTH-12	4,890	3/18/1997	--	HRS
PVTH-14	4,866	3/18/1997	--	HRS
PVTH-7	4,945	3/7/1997	--	HRS
PVTH-8	4,943	3/12/1997	--	HRS
S-10	4,721	1991–2001	--	CDWR
S-12	4,725	1990–1996, 1998–2001	10477-F	CDWR
S-18	4,706	1991–2001	--	CDWR
S-2	4,682	1990–96, 1998–2001	--	CDWR
S-23A	4,746	1994–1999, 2001	--	CDWR
S-24	4,681	1991–1994, 1996–2001	--	CDWR
S-26A	4,708	1993, 1995–96, 1998–2001	--	CDWR
S-3	4,698	1990–91, 1993–2001	31563-FP	CDWR

[1]Hydraulic head is average of observations on dates indicated.

Parameter Estimation

Sixteen parameters are used in the Lost Creek basin model, 10 of which were estimated by using inverse modeling methods. Parameters HK_1, HK_2, HK_3, HK_4, RCH_Nonirr, RCH_Flood, RCH_Sprink, Wells_PCC, Wells_Irr, and Q_Olds were estimated by using inverse methods. Parameters GHB_Out, GHB_In, GHB_Return, Q_Lord, GHB_Prspct, and EVT_Par were not estimated by inverse modeling methods because the relatively low sensitivity (see "Sensitivity Analysis") of these parameters prevented unique estimation of the parameters and convergence of the parameter-estimation process. Instead, these parameters were assigned reasonable values based on available data. The initial and final estimated parameter values used in the

model are shown in table 7. All final estimated parameter values appear reasonable compared to available data and estimated error associated with the data. Because the model is highly nonlinear (see "Model Nonlinearity"), linear confidence intervals are not presented for parameters.

Initial estimates of parameter values were assigned on the basis of data presented in the "Hydrogeology," "Recharge," and "Discharge" sections of this report, and parameter values were adjusted during model calibration. Initial estimates of HK_1, HK_2, and HK_3 are based on representative hydraulic-conductivity values estimated from aquifer-test and specific-capacity data presented in table 2. Because data were not available to estimate the value of HK_4, the initial parameter value was assigned a reasonable value without consideration of

Table 7. Initial and final parameter values, prior-information values, and prior-information weights used in the Lost Creek Designated Ground Water Basin model.

[ft/d, feet per day; ft²/d, square feet per day; acre-ft/acre/yr, acre-feet per acre per year; --, no value]

Parameter[1]	Model feature represented by parameter	Initial value	Final calibrated value	Prior-information value	Prior-information weight[2]	Units
HK_1	Horizontal hydraulic conductivity of zone 1	350	330	350	15	ft/d
HK_2	Horizontal hydraulic conductivity of zone 2	250	270	250	15	ft/d
HK_3	Horizontal hydraulic conductivity of zone 3	150	123	150	30	ft/d
HK_4	Horizontal hydraulic conductivity of zone 4	50	15	--	--	ft/d
RCH_Nonirr	Recharge rate beneath nonirrigated areas	0.7	1.5	0.9	0.2	in/yr
RCH_Flood	Recharge rate beneath flood-irrigated fields	4	8.2	4.9	1.2	in/yr
RCH_Sprink	Recharge rate beneath sprinkler-irrigated fields	2	3.4	2.4	1.2	in/yr
Wells_PCC	Withdrawal rate of irrigation wells with power-use data	−1.6	−1.5	−1.6	0.1	acre-ft/acre/yr
Wells_Irr	Withdrawal rate of irrigation wells lacking power-use data	−1.6	−0.94	−1.2	0.2	acre-ft/acre/yr
Q_Olds	Seepage rate of Olds Reservoir	0.14	0.19	0.14	0.02	ft/d
GHB_Out	Hydraulic conductance of the general-head boundary at the downgradient edge of the model	275,000	275,000	--	--	ft²/d
GHB_In	Hydraulic conductance of general-head boundaries at tributary valleys along the edge of the model	5,000	5,000	--	--	ft²/d
GHB_Return	Hydraulic conductance of the general-head boundary representing subsurface return flow along the west model boundary	5,000	5,000	--	--	ft²/d
Q_Lord	Seepage rate of Lord Reservoir	0.015	0.015	--	--	ft/d
GHB_Prspct	Hydraulic conductance of the general-head boundary at Prospect Reservoir	1,000	1,000	--	--	ft²/d
EVT_Par	Evapotranspiration rate	31	31	--	--	in/yr

[1]Parameters in bold were estimated by inverse methods.

[2]Prior-information weights represent assigned standard deviations of measurement error.

hydraulic-conductivity data. Final calibrated values of hydraulic-conductivity parameters (HK_1, HK_2, HK_3, and HK_4) range from 15 to 330 ft/d.

The initial estimate of RCH_Nonirr is based on average recharge values presented in table 3, assuming infiltration of water in ephemeral stream channels contributes about 5 percent of total recharge in nonirrigated areas. The final calibrated value of RCH_Nonirr is 1.5 in/yr. Initial estimates of RCH_Flood and RCH_Sprink are based on average recharge values for loam soils estimated by this study (table 4). Final calibrated values of RCH_Flood and RCH_Sprink are 8.2 in/yr and 3.4 in/yr, respectively. Although the final calibrated values of RCH_Nonirr, RCH_Flood, and RCH_Sprink are higher than initial estimates based on data collected during the study, the final values appear reasonable considering the potentially large variability and uncertainty associated with the parameters. The increased value of RCH_Nonirr is considered reasonable because it includes recharge from ephemeral streamflow and septic-system return flow of water withdrawn from bedrock aquifers underlying the Lost Creek basin, and both sources of recharge have substantial uncertainty. The increased values of RCH_Flood and RCH_Sprink are considered reasonable because the final values are within the range of values expected for deep-percolation return flow beneath irrigated fields, the initial estimates do not consider recharge from precipitation during the nonirrigation season, and recharge at the lysimeter locations may not be representative of recharge at other locations in the Lost Creek basin. Assuming average combined irrigation with surface water and

groundwater is 1.73 acre-ft/acre (20.8 inches) (see "Land Use and Irrigation") and long-term average annual precipitation is 14.1 inches, the final calibrated parameter value for RCH_Flood represents about 23 percent of applied water plus precipitation, and the final calibrated parameter value for RCH_Sprink represents about 10 percent of applied water plus precipitation. These ratios are within the range of values presented by other investigators, who estimated that about 49 percent (Susong, 1995) and 14–43 percent (Roark and Healy, 1998) of applied irrigation water plus precipitation became recharge beneath flood-irrigated fields and about 10 percent (Roark and Healy, 1998) to 12 percent (Gaggiani, 1995) of applied water plus precipitation became recharge beneath sprinkler-irrigated fields.

Initial estimates of Wells_PCC and Wells_Irr represent average withdrawal rates per acre of irrigated land based on data provided in Appendix 5. The final calibrated value of Wells_PCC is –1.5 acre-ft/acre/yr, and the final calibrated value of Wells_Irr is –0.94 acre-ft/acre/yr. The negative sign of the parameter values indicates water is withdrawn from the simulated aquifer rather than added. The downward adjustment of Wells_Irr from an initial estimated value of –1.6 acre-ft/acre/yr to –0.94 acre-ft/acre/yr is considered reasonable because the parameter represents average withdrawal rates for all irrigation wells lacking power-use data, whether or not the wells actually withdraw water in a given year. Because not all wells represented by parameter Wells_Irr might withdraw water in a given year, the average withdrawal rate can reasonably be expected to be less than if all wells were active.

The initial estimate of Q_Olds (0.14 ft/d) is based on the annually averaged seepage rate during 1990–2001 (table 5), and the initial estimate of Q_Lord (0.015 ft/d) is based on the annually averaged seepage rate during 1990–92. Final calibrated values of Q_Olds and Q_Lord are 0.19 ft/d and 0.015 ft/d, respectively. Parameter EVT_Par was assigned a value of about 31 in/yr. Hydraulic conductance of the general-head boundary representing groundwater outflow at the northern end of the Lost Creek basin (GHB_Out) was assigned a value of 275,000 ft²/d, and multipliers were used to adjust the hydraulic conductance of each cell represented by parameter GHB_Out to reflect variations in saturated thickness and hydraulic conductivity along the length of the boundary. Hydraulic conductances of general-head boundaries representing inflow from Prospect Reservoir (GHB_Prspct), tributary valleys at the edge of the model domain (GHB_In), and irrigation return flow along a part of the west model boundary (GHB_Return) were assigned values ranging from 1,000 to 5,000 ft²/d on the basis of estimated saturated thickness and hydraulic conductivity along the length of each boundary.

Calibration Assessment

The difference between an observation and a simulated value or between a prior-information value and a parameter estimate is called a residual. Overall model fit was evaluated with respect to residuals by using the standard error of the model regression and the fitted standard deviation of hydraulic head. The standard error of the regression is an indicator of the overall magnitude of weighted residuals and is provided as output from MODFLOW–2000. The standard error of the regression is expressed as (Hill, 1998):

$$s = \sqrt{\frac{S(\underline{b})}{(ND + NPR - NP)}} \qquad (8)$$

where

s is the standard error of the regression,

$S(\underline{b})$ is the value of the weighted least-squares objective function, calculated as

$$\sum_{i=1}^{ND} \omega_i[y_i - y'_i(\underline{b})]^2 + \sum_{p=1}^{NPR} \omega_p[P_p - P'_p(\underline{b})]^2$$

ND is the number of observations,

NPR is the number of prior-information values,

NP is the number of estimated parameters,

y_i is the ith observation being matched by the regression,

$y'_i(\underline{b})$ is the simulated value that corresponds to the ith observation (a function of $\underline{b}$),

P_p is the pth prior estimate included in the regression,

$P'_p(\underline{b})$ is the pth simulated value,

ω_i is the weight for the ith observation,

and

ω_p is the weight for the pth prior estimate.

Smaller values of standard error indicate better fit of simulated values to observations. The value of standard error should be close to 1.0 if weighting used on observations and prior information represents true data accuracy. In practice, standard error commonly is greater than 1.0 because of model error or greater-than-expected measurement error. The standard error of regression (table 8) for the calibrated model is 1.9.

The fitted standard deviation of hydraulic head is calculated by multiplying the standard error of the regression by the standard deviation of measurement error for hydraulic-head observations (Hill, 1998). Using a standard deviation of measurement error for hydraulic-head observations of 3 ft, the fitted standard deviation (overall fit) of hydraulic head in the model is 5.7 ft, which is about 0.7 percent of the total simulated head range in the model. Although the standard error of the model regression and fitted standard deviation of hydraulic head provide a general measure of model fit, they do not indicate the spatial distribution of error or the validity of the model regression (calibration).

A valid regression requires observation and prior-information errors used in the regression to be random and weighted errors to be uncorrelated (Draper and Smith, 1981). In addition, observation errors need to be normally distributed for use in calculating inferential statistics (Helsel and Hirsch, 1992) such as confidence intervals on parameters and predictions. If the model accurately represents the groundwater system and the foregoing conditions are met, weighted residuals should either be random, independent, and normal or have predictable correlations (Hill, 1998). To evaluate the randomness and independence of weighted residuals, weighted residuals are plotted relative to weighted simulated values (figs. 22A, B). For a valid regression, weighted residuals are randomly distributed above and below the zero line for all weighted simulated values (Draper and Smith, 1981). A nonrandom distribution or systematic trend in weighted residuals may indicate weighted residuals are not random or independent (Hill, 1994). The relation of weighted residuals to weighted simulated values for both hydraulic head and prior information are shown in figure 22A. Residuals in figure 22A plot in two general bands because the range of simulated hydraulic head values is different than the range of prior-information values. The

Table 8. Statistics used to assess calibration of the Lost Creek Designated Ground Water Basin model.

[Fitted standard deviation of hydraulic head in feet; all other values dimensionless]

Statistic	Value
Standard error of regression, s	1.9
Fitted standard deviation of hydraulic head	5.7
Minimum weighted hydraulic-head residual	−3.6
Maximum weighted hydraulic-head residual	4.3
Average weighted hydraulic-head residual	−0.03
Correlation coefficient, R^2_N	0.979
Critical value of R^2_N at the 5-percent significance level	0.956
Modified Beale's measure	2.7

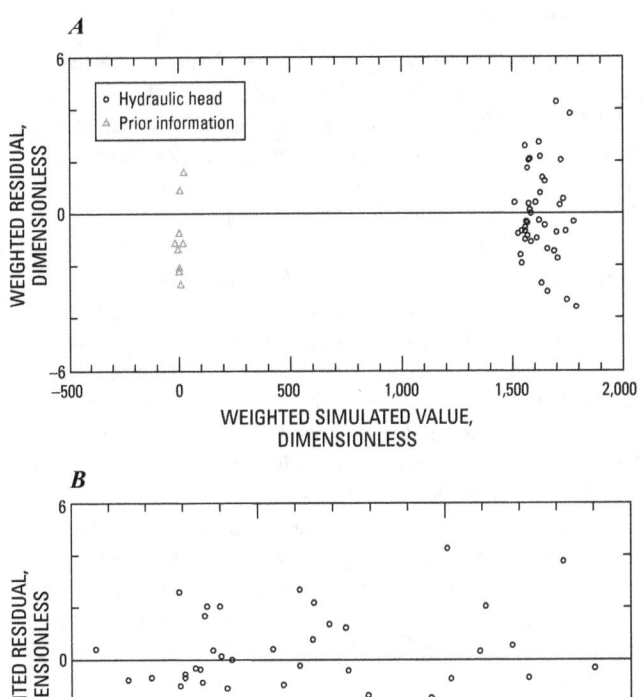

Figure 22. Relation of weighted residuals to weighted simulated values in the groundwater flow model for (*A*) hydraulic head and prior information and (*B*) hydraulic head only, Lost Creek Designated Ground Water Basin, Colorado.

relation of weighted residuals to weighted simulated values for hydraulic head only is shown in figure 22*B* to better illustrate the distribution of weighted hydraulic-head residuals. Because weighted residuals generally appear randomly distributed above and below the zero line for weighted simulated values in figures 22*A* and 22*B*, weighted residuals likely are nearly random and independent in the model. Slight divergence of weighted residuals relative to increasing weighted simulated values in figure 22*B* may indicate that simulated heads in the upgradient (southern) part of the basin do not match observed heads quite as well as in the downgradient (northern) part of the basin. A summary of the minimum, maximum, and average weighted hydraulic-head residual for the final calibrated model is presented in table 8.

To evaluate normality of weighted residuals and further test for their independence, a normal-probability graph of weighted residuals (fig. 23) was used. Because weighted residuals fall approximately on a straight line in the graph, weighted residuals may be considered independent and normally distributed. The correlation coefficient R^2_N provides another statistical

measure of residual independence and normality by determining the correlation between ordered weighted residuals and order statistics from a probability distribution function (Hill, 1998). If the value of R^2_N is significantly less than 1.0, weighted residuals are not likely to be independent and normally distributed. The value of R^2_N is calculated by MODFLOW–2000 and presented along with critical values for R^2_N representing significance levels of 0.05 and 0.10. The value of R^2_N for the final calibrated model is 0.979 (table 8) for observations and prior information, which is greater than the 5-percent significance level of 0.956 and indicates that the probability is greater than 95 percent that weighted residuals are independent and normally distributed.

Other statistical measures used to assess calibration of the final model are the runs statistic (Draper and Smith, 1981, p. 157–162) and the correlation between weighted observations and weighted simulated values. The runs statistic evaluates the spatial and temporal randomness of weighted residuals. A run consists of an unbroken sequence of positive or negative residuals. Too few or too many runs may indicate signifi-cant model error that could affect predictions (Hill, 1998). MODFLOW–2000 uses the order of observations listed in the observation input file to determine the runs statistic. The number of runs in the final calibrated model is 31 in 52 observa-tions (including prior information), which equals the number of runs expected and indicates that weighted residuals likely are randomly distributed in the model domain. Because the model is calibrated to steady-state conditions, temporal randomness is not considered. Correlation between weighted observations and weighted simulated values is evaluated by plotting weighted observations relative to weighted simulated values (figs. 24*A*, *B*). If weighted simulated values are similar to weighted obser-vations, points should fall on a straight line with an intercept of zero (Hill, 1998). Because the plots shown in figure 24 are approximately linear, weighted simulated values (and conse-quently, unweighted simulated values) can be considered to rea-sonably approximate weighted (and unweighted) observations.

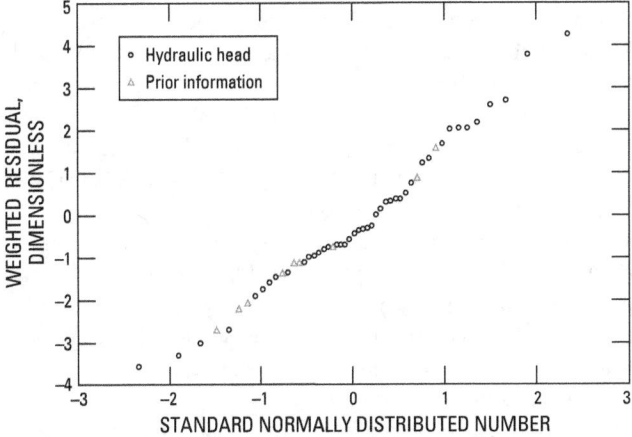

Figure 23. Normal probability plot of weighted residuals for the groundwater flow model, Lost Creek Designated Ground Water Basin, Colorado.

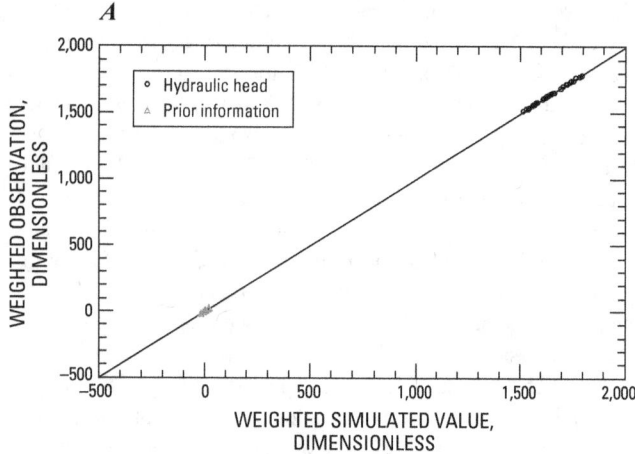

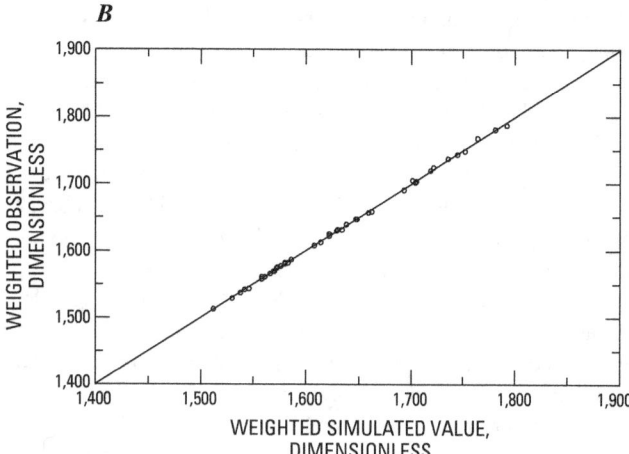

Figure 24. Relation of weighted observations to weighted simulated values in the groundwater flow model for (A) hydraulic head and prior information and (B) hydraulic head only, Lost Creek Designated Ground Water Basin, Colorado.

Parameter correlation coefficients indicate whether estimated parameter values are likely to be unique (Hill, 1998). Models calibrated to only hydraulic-head observations commonly have high parameter correlation, indicating problems with parameter uniqueness. Although the Lost Creek basin model is calibrated to only hydraulic head, parameter correlation coefficients for most estimated parameters in the final model are less than 0.85, indicating that most parameters likely could be uniquely estimated. One parameter pair (RCH_Flood and Wells_Irr) has a parameter correlation coefficient of –0.89, indicating that the two parameters were less likely independently estimated. The negative sign indicates that an increase in the estimate of RCH_Flood was correlated with a decrease (more negative, but greater magnitude) in the estimate of Wells_Irr.

Overall, calibration statistics indicate that simulated water levels generally have acceptable agreement with water levels measured at 43 locations in the Lost Creek basin. Hydraulic-head residuals likely are random, independent, and normal, indicating that the model regression likely is valid.

Sensitivity Analysis

Composite scaled sensitivities were calculated for each parameter using the Sensitivity Process (Hill and others, 2000) of MODFLOW–2000. Composite scaled sensitivities are dimensionless quantities that indicate the total amount of information provided by all observations for estimation of a parameter (Hill, 1998). When parameter correlation is not a problem, parameters with high sensitivity generally can be more precisely estimated from available observations than parameters with low sensitivity. Parameters with high sensitivity also have greater influence on hydraulic head simulated by the model and may be more important to accurately define for model simulations than parameters with low sensitivity. Parameters with very low sensitivity have little effect on simulated values, and accurate definition of these parameters is less important to model calibration. However, parameters with low sensitivity may be important to predictions if predictions are distant from observation locations or they differ in type (for example, flow rather than head) from the observations used to calibrate the model. Because composite scaled sensitivities depend on model structure and the number and location of observations, the absolute magnitude of composite scaled sensitivity for a parameter is less meaningful than its magnitude relative to that of other parameters. The composite scaled sensitivity of each parameter in the final calibrated model is presented in figure 25. The parameter representing withdrawals from irrigation wells lacking pumping data (Wells_Irr) has the highest composite scaled sensitivity in the model. Other parameters with relatively high composite scaled sensitivities represent recharge beneath nonirrigated areas (RCH_Nonirr) and recharge beneath flood-irrigated fields (RCH_Flood). Parameters with relatively low composite scaled sensitivities represent seepage from Lord Reservoir (Q_Lord), evapotranspiration (EVT_Par), and the hydraulic conductance of general-head boundaries simulating (1) seepage from Prospect Reservoir (GHB_Prspct), (2) subsurface return flow from ditches and irrigated fields located outside the model domain (GHB_Return), (3) subsurface inflow from tributary valleys (GHB_In), and (4) subsurface outflow at the north end of the Lost Creek basin (GHB_Out). Other model parameters have moderate sensitivity. Because parameter Wells_Irr, RCH_Nonirr, and RCH_Flood have the greatest composite scaled sensitivity, these parameters likely are the most important to accurately define for model simulations.

Model Nonlinearity

The postprocessing program BEALE–2000 (Hill and others, 2000) provided with MODFLOW–2000 is used to evaluate model nonlinearity. BEALE–2000 uses the modified Beale's measure (Cooley and Naff, 1990) to test model nonlinearity near the optimized parameter values. The model needs to be approximately linear for parameter values close to optimum parameter values for linear confidence intervals on predictions to be valid (Hill, 1994). Interpretation of the modified Beale's measure is different for each model and is provided as output by BEALE–2000. Results of BEALE–2000 indicate that the model can be considered effectively linear near optimized parameter values if the

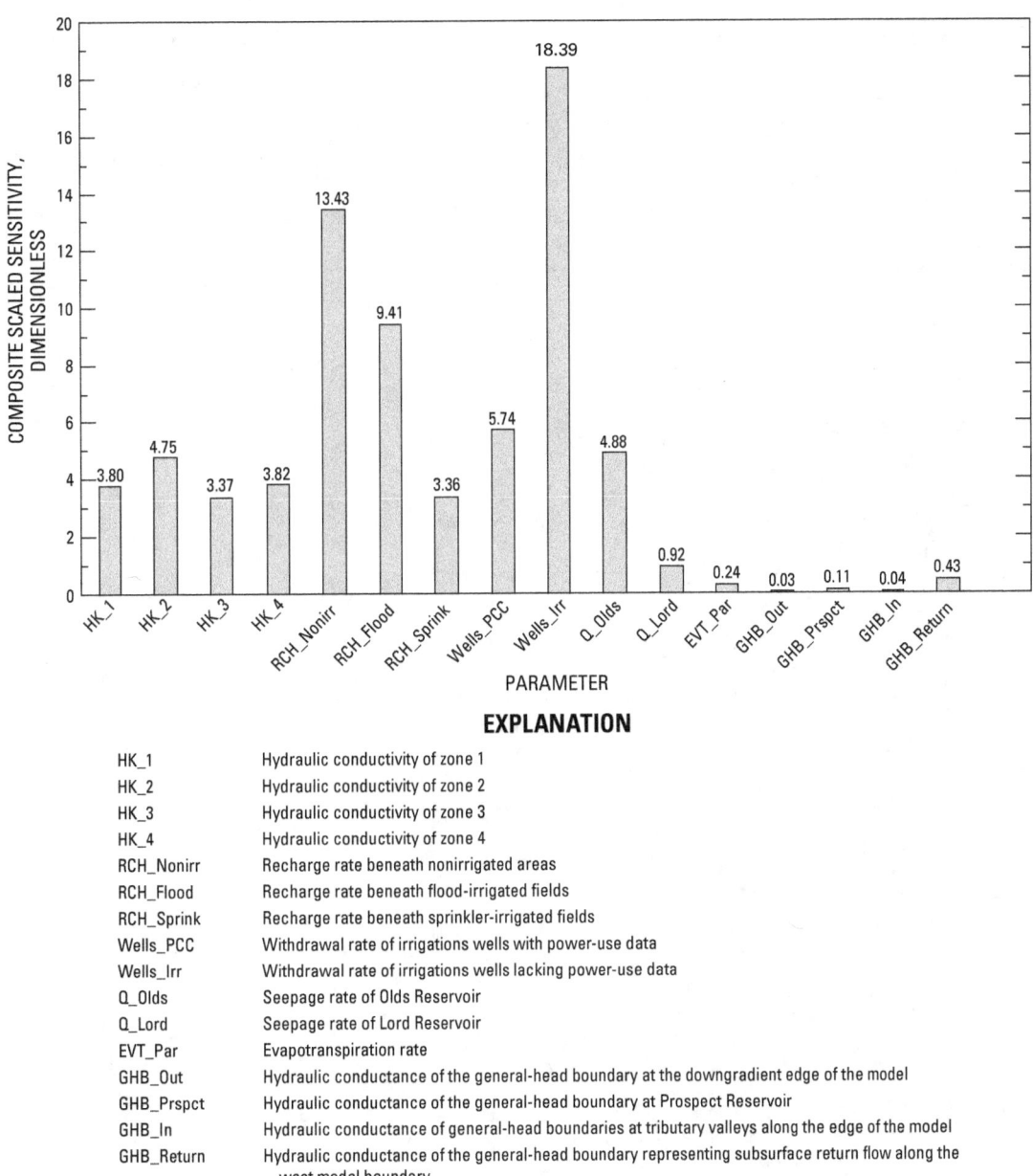

Figure 25. Composite scaled sensitivities of parameters in the groundwater flow model, Lost Creek Designated Ground Water Basin, Colorado.

Beale's measure is less than 0.043. The model can be considered intermediate if the Beale's measure is between 0.043 and 0.48 and nonlinear if it is greater than 0.48. Because the Beale's measure for the calibrated model is 2.7 (table 8), the model is considered nonlinear, and linear confidence intervals on parameters likely do not accurately represent parameter uncertainty. Similarly, linear confidence intervals on predictions made using the model likely would not accurately represent prediction uncertainty. The model is most nonlinear with respect to (1) sprinkler-irrigation recharge (RCH_Sprink), (2) flood-irrigated recharge (RCH_Flood), (3) seepage from Olds Reservoir (Q_Olds), and (4) withdrawals from irrigation wells lacking power-use data (Wells_Irr).

Simulation Results

The calibrated steady-state distribution of hydraulic head representing average water-table conditions in the Lost Creek basin during 1990–2001 is shown in figure 26. The simulated water table ranges in altitude from about 4,530 ft at the northern end of the Lost Creek basin to about 5,390 ft at the southern end of the basin. Groundwater in the simulated Lost Creek basin generally flows from the basin margins toward the center of the basin and northward along the main paleovalley of the basin. Water-table gradients range from about 10 ft/mi near Roggen to about 80 ft/mi in the southern part of the basin. Water-table gradients are flattest near Roggen because the main paleovalley in this area is

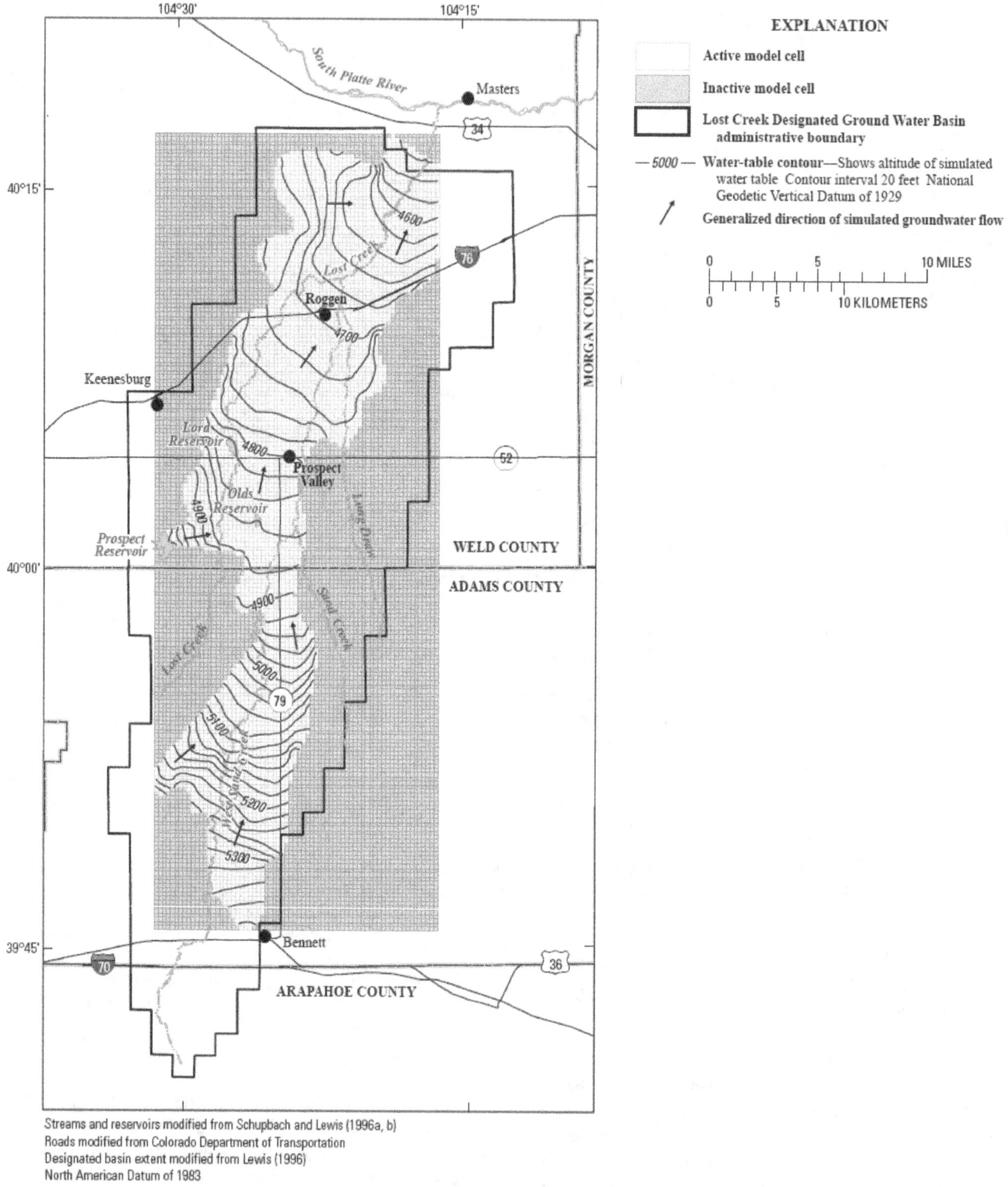

Streams and reservoirs modified from Schupbach and Lewis (1996a, b)
Roads modified from Colorado Department of Transportation
Designated basin extent modified from Lewis (1996)
North American Datum of 1983

Figure 26.   Steady-state altitude and configuration of the water table simulated by the groundwater flow model, Lost Creek Designated Ground Water Basin, Colorado.

wide, the bedrock surface is relatively flat, and aquifer transmissivity is high. Similarly, water-table gradients in the southern part of the basin are steepest because the main paleovalley in this area is comparatively narrow, the bedrock surface is relatively steep, and transmissivity is relatively low. Irregularities in the configuration of water-table contours are caused primarily by local variations in aquifer transmissivity, primarily as it relates to saturated thickness. Where transmissivity is relatively low, groundwater flow is impeded, and simulated hydraulic head is higher than in areas with greater transmissivity. Localized mounds in the water table near Olds and Lord Reservoirs are caused by simulated seepage from these reservoirs. Saturated thickness (fig. 27) in the model domain generally ranges from about 10 to 120 ft. Saturated thickness is greatest along the main paleovalley, especially in the northern part of the basin, where saturated thickness is as much as about 140 ft. Saturated thickness is least near basin margins and in areas of shallow bedrock, where saturated thickness can be less than 10 ft.

The computer program ZONEBUDGET (Harbaugh, 1990) was used to calculate the contribution of individual simulated components (such as recharge from nonirrigated areas, flood-irrigated fields, and sprinkler-irrigated fields) to the overall water budget (table 9). Combined recharge from deep percolation of water beneath flood- and sprinkler-irrigated agricultural fields (14,510 acre-ft/yr) is the largest source of inflow to the model, contributing 39.7 percent of the total inflow. Recharge from precipitation and stream-channel infiltration in nonirrigated areas (13,810 acre-ft/yr) is the second largest source of inflow to the model, contributing 37.7 percent of the total inflow. Other relatively substantial sources of inflow to the model are seepage from Olds Reservoir (4,280 acre-ft/yr) and subsurface inflow from ditches and irrigated fields outside the model domain (2,490 acre-ft/yr), which contribute 11.7 and 6.8 percent, respectively, of the total inflow. Inflow from small tributary valleys connected to the main Lost Creek basin paleovalley and seepage from Prospect and Lord Reservoirs collectively contribute 4.1 percent of the total inflow to the model. Irrigation well withdrawals (26,760 acre-ft/yr) are the largest source of outflow from the model, representing 73.2 percent of the total outflow. Groundwater discharge at the downgradient end of the Lost Creek basin (6,640 acre-ft/yr) represents 18.2 percent of the total outflow, and evapotranspiration (3,140 acre-ft/yr) represents 8.6 percent of the total outflow.

All values of the simulated water budget appear reasonable compared to available data. Although combined recharge from deep percolation of water beneath flood- and sprinkler-irrigated agricultural fields represents about 54 percent of irrigation-well withdrawals, this percentage does not consider other sources of water, such as surface-water irrigation and precipitation, that contribute to recharge beneath irrigated agricultural fields. Assuming surface-water irrigation is uniform, the amount of surface water applied to irrigated agricultural fields within the model domain (86.2 percent of the 32,500 acres irrigated acres in the Lost Creek basin, or 28,000 acres) is about 10,300 acre-ft (86.2 percent of the 11,900 acre-ft diverted to the Lost Creek basin), and water supplied to irrigated agricultural fields in the model domain by precipitation (14.1 in/yr, or about 1.18 acre-ft per acre) is about

32,900 acre-ft. When total water supplied to irrigated agricultural fields from groundwater, surface water, and precipitation are considered (69,960 acre-ft), total simulated recharge from deep percolation of water beneath irrigated fields represents about 21 percent of the total supplied water.

Model Limitations and Data Needs

Although the updated groundwater model presented in this report provides a reasonable representation of groundwater flow in the Lost Creek basin and statistics indicate the model is relatively well calibrated, the model is a simplified mathematical representation of a complex hydrologic system that is subject to limitations. The model cell size (1,000 ft × 1,000 ft) and level of detail are designed for simulating wide-scale aquifer responses to hydrologic stresses such as well withdrawals and changes in recharge. The model cannot accurately simulate aquifer responses to hydrologic stresses at a scale smaller than the model cell size. Because steady-state simulations represent average hydrologic conditions in the Lost Creek basin, short-term (seasonal) variations in hydrologic stresses are not considered, and use of the model for transient simulations might not accurately predict short-term hydrologic effects. Although calibration results indicate that most parameters likely were uniquely estimated, the addition of other types of observations, such as advective transport, could be useful to improving model calibration and reducing parameter correlation between the parameter representing recharge beneath flood-irrigated fields and the parameter representing withdrawals from wells lacking power-use data.

Several data needs were identified during this study that, if fulfilled, would improve hydrogeologic characterization of the Lost Creek basin and reduce model uncertainty as it relates to model input. Additional drilling or geophysical investigations could be undertaken to better define the saturated thickness and subsurface configuration of the Lost Creek basin in areas of little data or questionable data quality. In particular, additional hydrogeologic information would be useful to better define the hydrologic connection between the main Lost Creek paleovalley and the South Platte River valley and between the main paleovalley and Hay Gulch. Additional hydrogeologic information also would be useful to better define the configuration and thickness of the tributary paleovalley in the northwestern part of the study area and the main paleovalley in the southern part of the basin near the town of Bennett, particularly where saturated thickness is simulated as greater than 80 ft. Additional aquifer tests would be useful to better define the hydraulic properties of sediments in the southern part of the Lost Creek basin. Study of groundwater interaction between the Lost Creek basin and the underlying Denver Basin bedrock aquifers would be important to understanding the possible effects of groundwater withdrawals on flow between the aquifers. Monitoring of groundwater levels during the irrigation season as well as the nonirrigation season could provide for evaluation of the transient response of the aquifer to pumping and seasonal variations in recharge. Because simulated hydraulic head in the model is most sensitive to groundwater withdrawals from irrigation wells lacking power-use data, and withdrawals from these wells are not well quantified, additional evaluation of

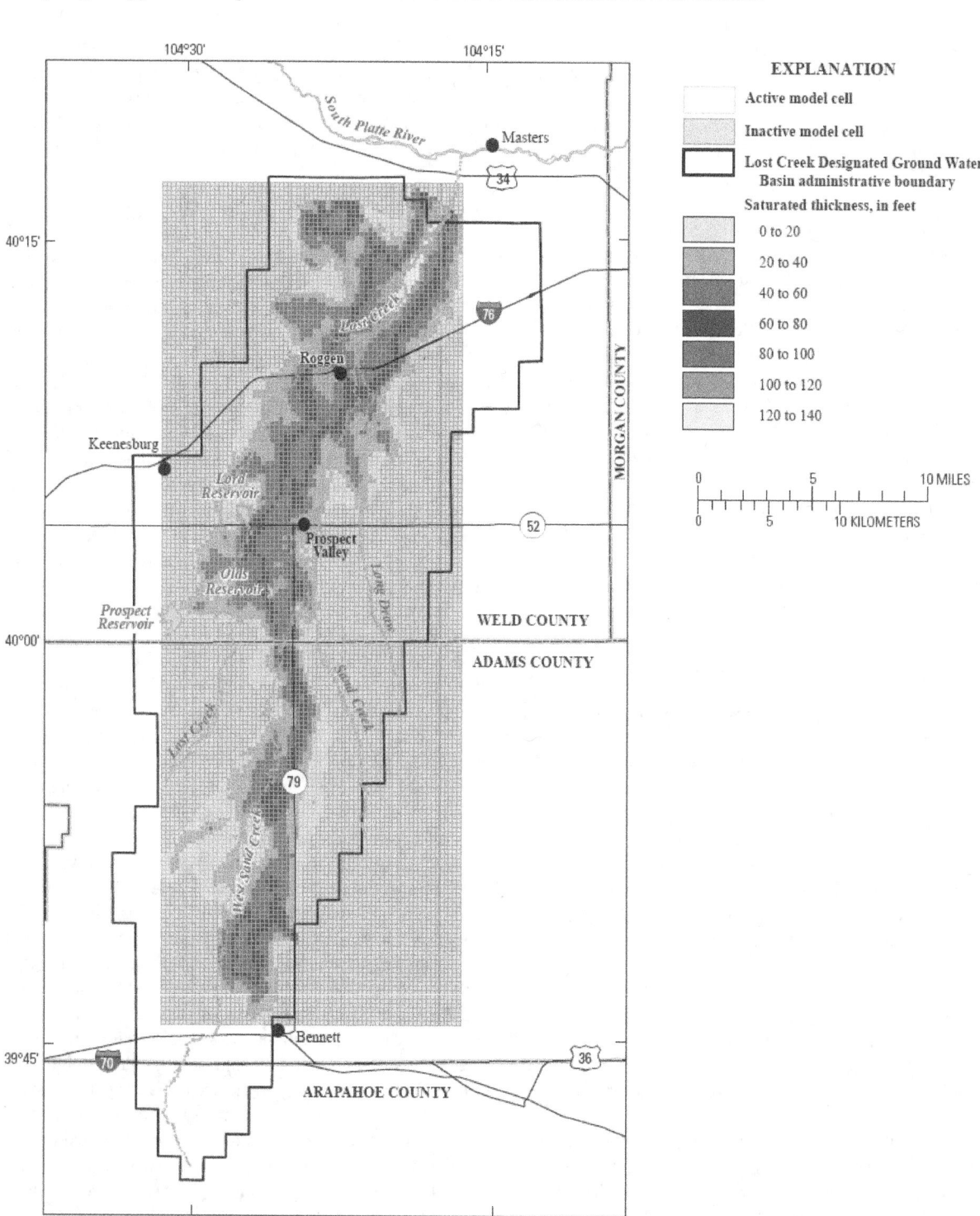

Streams and reservoirs modified from Schupbach and Lewis (1996a, b)
Roads modified from Colorado Department of Transportation
Designated basin extent modified from Lewis (1996)
North American Datum of 1983

Figure 27.   Saturated thickness simulated by the groundwater flow model, Lost Creek Designated Ground Water Basin, Colorado.

Table 9. Simulated steady-state groundwater budget of the Lost Creek Designated Ground Water Basin model representing conditions for 1990–2001.

[ft³/d, cubic feet per day; acre-ft, acre-feet]

Budget component	Flow rate (ft³/d)	Annual flow volume (acre-ft)	Percentage of total inflow or outflow
Inflows[1]			
Recharge from precipitation and stream-channel infiltration in nonirrigated areas	1,648,000	13,810	37.7
Recharge from deep percolation of water beneath flood-irrigated agricultural fields	1,162,000	9,740	26.6
Recharge from deep percolation of water beneath sprinkler-irrigated agricultural fields	569,600	4,770	13.1
Groundwater inflow from small tributary valleys	35,100	290	0.8
Groundwater inflow from ditches and irrigated fields outside the model domain	297,100	2,490	6.8
Seepage from Prospect Reservoir	37,800	320	0.9
Seepage from Olds Reservoir	510,800	4,280	11.7
Seepage from Lord Reservoir	105,600	890	2.4
Total	4,366,000	36,590	100.0
Outflows[1]			
Irrigation well withdrawals	3,193,000	26,760	73.2
Groundwater outflow at downgradient end of the Lost Creek Designated Ground Water Basin	792,800	6,640	18.2
Evapotranspiration	375,100	3,140	8.6
Total	4,360,900	36,540	100.0
Percent discrepancy[2] (Inflows–Outflows)	0.1	0.1	

[1]Inflows and outflows are net values (flow into minus flow out of cells representing each budget component).

[2]Percent discrepancy represents error due to the limited precision of the solution to the finite-difference equations used by the model.

well withdrawals would be important to improving simulations of groundwater flow in the Lost Creek basin and reducing model uncertainty. Estimates of recharge to the Lost Creek basin could be improved by additional study of deep-percolation return flow beneath flood- and sprinkler-irrigated fields and by detailed investigation of seepage loss along ditches in the Henrylyn irrigation system in the Lost Creek basin.

Summary

The Lost Creek Designated Ground Water Basin (Lost Creek basin) is an important alluvial aquifer for irrigation, public supply, and domestic water uses in northeastern Colorado. Urban growth in the adjacent Front Range urban corridor has increased demand for groundwater in the basin, and potential exportation of groundwater from the basin has raised concerns about the long-term sustainability and management of the basin's groundwater resources. Beginning in 2005 the U.S. Geological Survey, in cooperation with the Lost Creek Ground Water Management District and the Colorado Water Conservation Board, collected hydrologic data and constructed a numerical groundwater flow model of the Lost Creek basin. The steady-state model builds upon the work of previous investigators to provide an updated tool for simulating the potential effects of various hydrologic stresses on groundwater flow and evaluating possible aquifer-management strategies.

Development of the Lost Creek basin model included (1) mapping the thickness and extent of regolith sediments to define the subsurface configuration of the Lost Creek basin and (2) collecting data related to infiltration of precipitation and

stream channels, deep percolation of water applied to irrigated agricultural fields, ditch and reservoir seepage, and subsurface inflow to improve estimates of recharge to the basin. Data concerning well withdrawals, evapotranspiration, and subsurface outflow were used to estimate discharge from the basin.

The thickness and extent of regolith sediments indicate a well-defined paleovalley that extends along the Lost Creek basin from south to north, where it joins the alluvial valley of the South Platte River. Regolith along the main part of the paleovalley is as much as about 190 ft thick, and several smaller paleovalleys appear tributary to the main paleovalley that have regolith as much as 120 ft thick.

Recharge from infiltration of precipitation on native grassland and nonirrigated agricultural fields was estimated by using the chloride mass-balance method at four sites in the Lost Creek basin. Recharge from infiltration of ephemeral streamflow was estimated by using apparent downward velocities of chloride peaks in soil profiles at two sites located in the stream channels of West Sand Creek and Long Draw. Recharge from deep percolation of water applied to irrigated agricultural fields was estimated by using passive-wick lysimeters installed at four sites in the Lost Creek basin and by using a water-balance approach.

Average annual recharge from infiltration of precipitation on native grassland and nonirrigated agricultural fields was estimated to range from 0.1 to 0.6 inch, which represents about 1–4 percent of long-term average precipitation. Average annual recharge from infiltration of ephemeral streamflow in the channels of West Sand Creek and Long Draw was estimated to range from 5.7 to 8.2 inches over the area of the stream channels.

Recharge from deep percolation of water applied to irrigated agricultural fields varied by irrigation method, soil type, crop type, and the net quantity of irrigation water applied. Recharge estimated by lysimeter drainage at a sprinkler-irrigated alfalfa field on loam soil ranged from 1.0 to 1.8 inches during the irrigation season and represented 5–7 percent of net irrigation and 4–6 percent of net irrigation plus precipitation. Recharge estimated by lysimeter drainage at a sprinkler-irrigated field on sandy soil ranged from 3.0 to 4.0 inches during the irrigation season for corn and alfalfa crops and represented 23–30 percent of net irrigation and 17–26 percent of net irrigation plus precipitation. Recharge estimated by lysimeter drainage beneath flood-irrigated fields on loam soil ranged from 0.1 to 3.5 inches during the irrigation season for wheat and corn crops and represented 13–20 percent of net irrigation and 5–11 percent of net irrigation plus precipitation. Because of the potential variability of net irrigation over the area of flood-irrigated fields, recharge estimates for flood-irrigated fields have larger uncertainty than recharge estimates for sprinkler-irrigated fields.

Recharge estimated by using a water-balance method had a wider range of values than recharge estimated by lysimeter drainage, likely because recharge estimated by the water-balance method was sensitive to inaccuracies in the estimates of other water-balance components. Recharge estimated using the water-balance method at a sprinkler-irrigated field on loam soil ranged from 0 to 5.0 inches, which represented 0–19 percent of net irrigation and 0–16 percent of net irrigation plus precipitation. Recharge estimated by using the water-balance method at a sprinkler-irrigated field on sandy soil indicated no recharge occurred during the period of study because cumulative evapotranspiration exceeded cumulative net irrigation plus precipitation. Recharge estimated by the water-balance method at flood-irrigated fields on loam soil ranged from 0 to 11.3 inches, which represented 0–43 percent of net irrigation and 0–37 percent of net irrigation plus precipitation.

The USGS modular groundwater modeling program, MODFLOW–2000, was used to develop a steady-state groundwater flow model of the Lost Creek basin. The model primarily was calibrated to average hydrologic conditions representing the period 1990–2001 by using the Observation, Sensitivity, and Parameter-Estimation Processes of MODFLOW–2000. Forty-three hydraulic-head observations were used to calibrate the model. Because perennial streams do not exist in the Lost Creek basin, the model was not calibrated to flow observations representing streamflow gains or losses. Sixteen parameters were used in the model, 10 of which were estimated by using inverse modeling methods. Simulated water levels generally have acceptable agreement with measured water levels, and calibration statistics indicate that residuals between simulated and measured values of hydraulic head likely are random, independent, and normally distributed.

The parameter representing withdrawals from irrigation wells lacking pumping data had the highest composite scaled sensitivity in the model. Other parameters with relatively high composite scaled sensitivities represent recharge beneath nonirrigated areas and recharge beneath flood-irrigated fields. Because composite scaled sensitivities were highest for parameters representing withdrawals from wells lacking pumping data, recharge beneath nonirrigated areas, and recharge beneath flood-irrigated fields, these parameters likely are the most important to accurately define for model simulations.

Groundwater in the simulated Lost Creek basin generally flows from the basin margins toward the center of the basin and northward along the main paleovalley of the basin. Water-table gradients range from about 10 ft/mi near Roggen to about 80 ft/mi in the southern part of the basin. Water-table gradients are flattest near Roggen because the main paleovalley in this area is wide, the bedrock surface is relatively flat, and aquifer transmissivity is high. Water-table gradients in the southern part of the basin are steepest because the main paleovalley in this area is comparatively narrow, the bedrock surface is relatively steep, and transmissivity is low. Saturated thickness in the model domain ranges from less than 10 to about 140 ft. Saturated thickness is greatest along the main paleovalley, especially in the northern part of the basin. Saturated thickness is least near basin margins and in areas of shallow bedrock.

The largest source of inflow to the model domain occurs from recharge beneath flood- and sprinkler-irrigated agricultural fields (14,510 acre-ft/yr), which represents 39.7 percent of total simulated inflow. Other substantial sources of inflow to the model domain are recharge by precipitation and stream-channel infiltration in nonirrigated areas (13,810 acre-ft/yr), seepage from Olds Reservoir (4,280 acre-ft/yr), and subsurface inflow from ditches and irrigated fields outside the model domain (2,490 acre-ft/yr), which contribute 37.7, 11.7, and 6.8 percent, respectively, of total inflow. The largest outflow from the model occurs from irrigation well withdrawals (26,760 acre-ft/yr), which represent 73.2 percent of total outflow. Groundwater discharge (6,640 acre-ft/yr) at the downgradient end of the Lost Creek basin represents 18.2 percent of total outflow, and evapotranspiration (3,140 acre-ft/yr) represents 8.6 percent of total outflow.

Acknowledgments

Many individuals contributed to this study. Thanks are extended to all landowners who granted access to their properties for the collection of data. Special thanks go to Rich Huwa, Dave and Paul Rupple, and Steve Bruntz for allowing installation of lysimeters to measure deep percolation beneath their irrigated agricultural fields. Thanks also are extended to Tom Sauter, John Cordes, Rich Huwa, Steven Deutch, Steven Jansen, and Woody Eppelsheimer for providing valuable information about farming practices, hydrologic conditions, and water development in the Lost Creek basin. Rod Baumgartner of the Henrylyn Irrigation District provided important irrigation data, and his contribution is gratefully acknowledged. Technical support provided by Rick Healy (USGS National Research Program) concerning the collection and analysis of data used to estimate recharge also is gratefully acknowledged.

References Cited

Allison, G.B., Gee, G.W., and Tyler, S.W., 1994, A review of vadose-zone techniques for estimating groundwater recharge in arid and semiarid regions: Soil Science Society of America Journal, v. 58, p. 63–72.

Allison, G.B., and Hughes, M.W., 1978, The use of environmental chloride and tritium to estimate total recharge to an unconfined aquifer: Australian Journal of Soil Research, v. 16, p. 181–195.

Argus Interware, 1997, Argus ONE user's guide, Argus Open Numerical Environments—A GIS Modeling System, version 4.0: Jericho, N.Y., Argus Holdings, Limited, 320 p.

Arnold, L.R., 2010, Geographic information system datasets of regolith-thickness data, regolith-thickness contours, raster-based regolith thickness, and aquifer-test and specific-capacity data for the Lost Creek Designated Ground Water Basin, Weld, Adams, and Arapahoe Counties, Colorado: U.S. Geological Survey Data Series 507.

Bjorklund, L.J., and Brown, R.F., 1957, Geology and ground-water resources of the lower South Platte River valley between Hardin, Colorado, and Paxton, Nebraska: U.S. Geological Survey Water-Supply Paper 1378, 431 p., 4 pls.

Braddock, W.A., and Cole, J.C., 1978, Preliminary geologic map of the Greeley 1°×2° quadrangle, Colorado and Wyoming: U.S. Geological Survey Open-File Report 78–532, scale 1:250,000.

Bryant, B., McGrew, L.W., and Wobus, R.A., 1981, Geologic map of the Denver 1°×2° quadrangle, north-central Colorado: U.S. Geological Survey Miscellaneous Investigations Series Map I–1163, 2 sheets, scale 1:250,000.

Code, W.E., 1945, Ground water supply of Prospect Valley, Colorado: Colorado Agricultural Experiment Station Technical Bulletin 34, 40 p.

Coes, A.L., and Pool, D.R., 2005, Ephemeral stream-channel and basin-floor infiltration and recharge in the Sierra Vista sub-watershed of the Upper San Pedro Basin, southeastern Arizona: U.S. Geological Survey Open-File Report 2005–1023, 67 p.

Colorado Division of Water Resources, 2000, Ground water levels in the Lost Creek Designated Ground Water Basin 2000: Colorado Division of Water Resources, Denver, Colo.

Colorado Division of Water Resources, 2007, CDSS climate stations, Division 1, database version 20070901: Colorado's Decision Support Systems spatial dataset available on the Web, accessed May 30, 2008, at *http://cdss.state.co.us/ DNN/GIS/tabid/67/Default.aspx.*

Colorado Division of Water Resources, 2008, Colorado's Decision Support Systems: Colorado Division of Water Resources diversion data available on the Web, accessed February 20, 2008, at *http://cdss.state.co.us/DNN/ Structures/tabid/75/Default.aspx.*

Cooley, R.L., and Naff, R.L., 1990, Regression modeling of ground-water flow: U.S. Geological Survey Techniques of Water-Resources Investigations, book 3, chap. B4, 232 p.

Dane, J.H., and Topp, G.C., eds., 2002, Methods of soil analysis, part 4, Physical methods: Madison, Wis., Soil Science Society of America Book Series, v. 5, 866 p.

DeMeo, G.A., Smith, J.L., Damar, N.A., and Darnell, J., 2008, Quantifying ground-water and surface-water discharge from evapotranspiration processes in 12 hydrographic areas of the Colorado Regional Groundwater Flow System, Nevada, Utah, and Arizona: U.S. Geological Survey Scientific Investigations Report 2008–5116, 22 p.

Draper, N.R., and Smith, H., 1981, Applied regression analysis (2d ed.): New York, John Wiley, 709 p.

Fenneman, N.M., 1946, Physical divisions of the United States: U.S. Geological Survey map, scale 1:7,000,000.

Fetter, C.W., 1994, Applied hydrogeology (3d ed.): New York, Prentice-Hall, 691 p.

Gaggiani, N.G., 1995, Ground-water flow and effects of agricultural applications of sewage sludge and other fertilizers on the chemical quality of sediments in the unsaturated zone and ground water near Platteville, Colorado, 1985–89: U.S. Geological Survey Water-Resources Investigations Report 94–4037, 41 p.

Gee, G.W., Ward, A.L., Caldwell, T.G., and Ritter, J.C., 2002, A vadose zone water fluxmeter with divergence control: Water Resources Research, v. 38, no. 8, p. 16–1—16–7.

Glover, R.E., 1959, Ground water recharge in Prospect Valley, Colorado—Part I, Analytical studies: Colorado Agricultural Experiment Station Research Project 112, Preliminary Progress Report, 25 p.

Harbaugh, A.W., 1990, A computer program for calculating subregional water budgets using results from the U.S. Geological Survey modular three-dimensional finite-difference ground-water flow model: U.S. Geological Survey Open-File Report 90–392, 46 p.

Harbaugh, A.W., Banta, E.R., Hill, M.C., and McDonald, M.C., 2000, MODFLOW–2000, the U.S. Geological Survey modular ground-water model—User guide to modularization concepts and the ground-water flow process: U.S. Geological Survey Open-File Report 2000–92, 121 p.

Heil, R.D., Moreland, D.C., Cipra, J.E., Phillips, J.R., and Williams, R.D., 1978, Soil resources of Colorado Region 2—Larimer and Weld Counties: Colorado State University Experiment Station Special Series no. 1, 141 p., 3 pls.

Helsel, D.R., and Hirsch, R.M., 1992, Statistical methods in water resources: Elsevier, 522 p.

Hill, M.C., 1990, Preconditioned conjugate-gradient 2 (PCG2), a computer program for solving ground-water flow equations: U.S. Geological Survey Water-Resources Investigations Report 90–4048, 43 p.

Hill, M.C., 1994, Five computer programs for testing weighted residuals and calculating linear confidence and prediction intervals on results from the ground-water parameter estimation computer program MODFLOWP: U.S. Geological Survey Open-File Report 93–481, 81 p.

Hill, M.C., 1998, Methods and guidelines for effective model calibration: U.S. Geological Survey Water-Resources Investigations Report 98–4005, 90 p.

Hill, M.C., Banta, E.R., Harbaugh, A.W., and Anderman, E.R., 2000, MODFLOW-2000, the U.S. Geological Survey modular ground-water model—User guide to the Observation, Sensitivity, and Parameter-Estimation Processes and three post-processing programs: U.S. Geological Survey Open-File Report 2000–184, 209 p.

Hurr, R.T., Schneider, P.A., Jr., and others, 1972, Hydrogeologic characteristics of the valley-fill aquifer in the Weldona reach of the South Platte River valley, Colorado: U.S. Geological Survey Open-File Report 73–127, 2 p. 6 pl.

Jensen, M.E., Burman, R.D., and Allen, R.G., eds., 1990, Evapotranspiration and irrigation water requirements: American Society of Civil Engineers Manuals and Reports on Engineering Practice no. 70, 332 p.

Jones, P.A, and Cech, T.C., 2009, Colorado Water Law: Boulder, University Press of Colorado, 276 p.

Lewis, L.E., 1996, Designated basin: Colorado Division of Water Resources spatial dataset available on the Web, accessed May 30, 2008, at *http://water.state.co.us/pubs/gis.asp.*

Maurer, D.K., and Thodal, C.E., 2000, Quantity and chemical quality of recharge, and updated water budgets, for the basin-fill aquifer in Eagle Valley, western Nevada: U.S. Geological Survey Water-Resources Investigations Report 99–4289, 46 p.

McDonald, M.G., and Harbaugh, A.W., 1988, A modular three-dimensional finite-difference ground-water flow model: U.S. Geological Survey Techniques of Water-Resources Investigations, book 6, chap. A1, 586 p.

McMahon, P.B., Dennehy, K.F., Michel, R.L., Sophocleous, M.A., Ellett, K.M., and Hurlbut, D.B., 2003, Water movement through thick unsaturated zones overlying the central High Plains aquifer, southwestern Kansas, 2000–2001: U.S. Geological Survey Water-Resources Investigations Report 2003–4171, 32 p.

National Atmospheric Deposition Program, 2005, Atmospheric deposition data on the Web, accessed November 21, 2005 at *http://nadp.sws.uiuc.edu/sites/ntnmap.asp.*

Nelson, Haley, Patterson, and Quirk, Inc., 1967, Ground water resources of the Lost Creek drainage basin, Weld, Adams, and Arapahoe Counties, Colorado: Report prepared for the Colorado Ground Water Commission, 32 p., 3 pls.

Prudic, D.E., 1991, Estimates of hydraulic conductivity from aquifer-test analyses and specific-capacity data, Gulf Coast regional aquifer systems, south-central United States: U.S. Geological Survey Water-Resources Investigations Report 90–4121, 38 p.

Riverside Technology, Inc., 2006, SPDSS, 2001 Division 1 ditch service areas: Colorado's Decision Support Systems spatial dataset available on the Web, accessed May 30, 2008, at *http://cdss.state.co.us/DNN/GIS/tabid/67/Default.aspx.*

Riverside Technology, Inc., 2007, South Platte Decision Support System, Division 1 irrigated lands, 2001: Colorado's Decision Support Systems spatial dataset available on the Web, accessed May 30, 2008, at *http://cdss.state.co.us/DNN/GIS/tabid/67/Default.aspx.*

Roark, D.M., and Healy, D.F., 1998, Quantification of deep percolation from two flood-irrigated alfalfa fields, Roswell Basin, New Mexico: U.S. Geological Survey Water-Resources Investigations Report 98–4096, 32 p.

Robinson, T.W., 1958, Phreatophytes: U.S. Geological Survey Water-Supply Paper 1423, 84 p.

Robson, S.G., 1983, Hydraulic characteristics of the principal bedrock aquifers in the Denver Basin, Colorado: U.S. Geological Survey Hydrologic Investigations Atlas HA–659, 3 sheets, scale 1:500,000.

Robson, S.G., 1987, Bedrock aquifers in the Denver Basin, Colorado—A quantitative water-resources appraisal: U.S. Geological Survey Professional Paper 1257, 73 p.

Scanlon, B.R., Keese, K.E., Flint, A.L., Flint, L.E., Gaye, C.B., Edmunds, W.M., and Simmers, I., 2006, Global synthesis of groundwater recharge in semiarid and arid regions: Hydrological Processes, v. 20, p. 3335–3370.

Schaubs, M.P., 2007, Ground water levels in the Lost Creek Designated Ground Water Basin 2007: Colorado Division of Water Resources, Denver, Colorado, 10 p.

Schupbach, S.A., and Lewis, L.E., 1995, Denver Basin aquifer boundaries: Colorado Division of Water Resources spatial dataset available on the Web, accessed May 30, 2008, at *http://water.state.co.us/pubs/gis.asp.*

Schupbach, S.A., and Lewis, L.E., 1996a, CDSS lakes Division 1: Colorado's Decision Support Systems spatial dataset available on the Web, accessed May 30, 2008 at *http://cdss.state.co.us/DNN/GIS/tabid/67/Default.aspx.*

Schupbach, S.A., and Lewis, L.E., 1996b, CDSS rivers Division 1: Colorado's Decision Support Systems spatial dataset available on the Web, accessed May 30, 2008 at *http://cdss.state.co.us/DNN/GIS/tabid/67/Default.aspx.*

Skinner, M.M., 1963, Artificial ground-water recharge in the Prospect Valley area, Colorado: Colorado Agricultural Experiment Station General Series 792, 89 p.

Stonestrom, D.A., Prudic, D.E., Laczniak, R.J., Akstin, K.C., Boyd, R.A., and Henkelman, K.K., 2003, Estimates of deep percolation beneath native vegetation, irrigated fields, and the Amargosa River channel, Amargosa Desert, Nye County, Nevada: U.S. Geological Survey Open-File Report 2003–104, 88 p.

Susong, D.D., 1995, Water budget and simulation of one-dimensional unsaturated flow for a flood- and a sprinkler-irrigated field near Milford, Utah: U.S. Geological Survey Water-Resources Investigations Report 95–4072, 32 p.

Theis, C.V., Brown, R.H., and Meyer, R.R., 1963, Estimating the transmissibility of aquifers from the specific capacities of wells, *in* Bentall, Ray, 1963, Methods of determining permeability, transmissibility and drawdown: U.S. Geological Survey Water-Supply Paper 1536–I, p. 331–341.

Thorn, C.R., 1995, Surface-water discharge and evapotranspiration rates for grass and bare soil along a reach of the Rio Grande, Albuquerque, New Mexico, 1989–95: U.S. Geological Survey Open-File Report 95–419, 23 p.

U.S. Department of Agriculture, Natural Resources Conservation Service, 1994, CDSS soils, Division 1: Colorado's Decision Support Systems spatial dataset available on the Web, accessed May 30, 2008, at *http://cdss.state.co.us/DNN/GIS/tabid/67/Default.aspx.*

U.S. Geological Survey, 2000, CDSS National Land Cover Dataset, Division 1: Colorado's Decision Support Systems spatial dataset available on the Web, accessed May 30, 2008, at *http://cdss.state.co.us/DNN/GIS/tabid/67/Default.aspx.*

U.S. Geological Survey, 2002, 1/3-Arc Second National Elevation Dataset: U.S Geological Survey raster digital data available on the Web, accessed February 15, 2008, at *http://seamless.usgs.gov.*

Western Regional Climate Center, 2008, Historical climate information: Western Regional Climate Center data available on the Web, accessed May 23, 2008, at http://*www.wrcc.dri.edu/CLIMATEDATA.html.*

Wilson, W.W., 1965, Pumping tests in Colorado: Denver, Colorado Water Conservation Board Ground Water Circular 11, 361 p.

Winston, R.B., 2000, Graphical user interface for MODFLOW, version 4: U.S. Geological Survey Open-File Report 2000–0315, 27 p.

Wood, W.W., 1999, Use and misuse of the chloride-mass balance method in estimating ground water recharge: Ground Water, v. 37, no. 1, p. 2–3.

Appendixes

Appendix 1. Gravimetric water content and chloride concentrations for soil samples collected in 2006 at six sites in the Lost Creek Designated Ground Water Basin.

[ft, feet; g/g, grams of water per gram of dry sediment; µg/g, micrograms of chloride per gram of dry sediment; mg/L, milligrams of chloride per liter of water]

Site	Latitude	Longitude	Sample depth (ft)	Gravimetric water content (g/g)	Chloride concentration[1] (µg/g)	Chloride concentration[1] (mg/L)
C1	39 52'01.8"	104 27'41.0"	2	0.100	2.96	29.6
			4	0.062	8.66	140
			6	0.013	7.70	592
			8	0.026	6.47	249
			10	0.022	1.42	64.5
			12	0.045	0.55	12.2
			14	0.034	0.20	5.88
			16	0.074	0.32	4.32
			17	0.241	0.42	1.74
			18	0.225	0.39	1.73
			20	0.268	0.67	2.50
C2	39 52'01.7"	104 27'42.4"	2	0.030	0.86	28.7
			4	0.043	1.52	35.3
			6	0.091	2.50	27.5
			8	0.093	0.77	8.28
			10	0.244	0.72	2.95
			12	0.258	3.71	14.4
			14	0.247	1.02	4.13
			16	0.213	3.37	15.8
			18	0.302	2.33	7.72
			20	0.146	1.44	9.86
C3	39 55'35.0"	104 23'59.5"	2	0.183	5.49	30.0
			4	0.179	3.45	19.3
			6	0.178	1.85	10.4
			8	0.144	4.20	29.2
			10	0.176	63.5	361
			12	0.160	66.5	416
			14	0.182	213	1,170
			16	0.134	312	2,330
			18	0.045	77.5	1,722
			20	0.028	70.6	2,480
C4	40 00'03.0"	104 27'06.9"	2	0.132	2.38	18.0
			4	0.110	1.47	13.4
			6	0.123	2.00	16.3
			8	0.130	7.29	56.1
			10	0.167	1.50	8.98
			12	0.085	2.08	24.5
			14	0.158	3.93	24.9
			16	0.196	9.32	47.6
			18	0.195	4.38	22.5
			20	0.223	2.58	11.6
C5	40 06'06.2"	104 21'24.4"	2	0.063	2.06	32.7
			4	0.079	1.28	16.2
			6	0.111	6.16	55.5
			8	0.158	19.0	120
			10	0.209	3.82	18.3
			12	0.230	6.84	29.7
			14	0.180	3.63	20.2
			16	0.212	2.14	10.1
			18	0.243	2.26	9.30
			20	0.206	1.41	6.84
C6	40 06'06.3"	104 21'23.5"	2	0.133	0.85	6.39
			4	0.121	1.62	13.4
			6	0.124	1.21	9.76
			8	0.173	1.71	9.88
			10	0.176	9.32	53.0
			12	0.206	2.21	10.7
			14	0.244	15.7	64.5
			16	0.213	2.67	12.5
			18	0.231	4.83	20.9
			20	0.118	5.98	50.7

[1]Chloride concentrations are the average value of any duplicate samples from the same depth. The chloride concentration of each duplicate sample is presented in Appendix 2.

Appendix 2.   Analytical quality-assurance and quality-control data for soil samples collected in 2006 at six sites in the Lost Creek Designated Ground Water Basin, Colorado

[μg/g, micrograms of chloride per gram of sediment; mg/L, milligrams of chloride per liter of water; Relative % Diff., the difference between duplicate or replicate analyses divided by the average of the analyses and expressed as percent; Grand Avg. Precision, the average of Relative % Diff. for all duplicate samples]

Site[1]	Depth (ft)	Quality-control sample	Chloride concentration (μg/g)	Chloride concentration (mg/L)
		Bias		
Minimum reporting limit				0.06
Maximum reporting limit				3,526
C1		Deionized water 1		< 0.06
		Deionized water 2		< 0.06
		Deionized water 3		< 0.06
		Blank 1		< 0.06
		Blank 2		< 0.06
C2		Deionized water 1		< 0.06
		Deionized water 2		< 0.06
		Blank 1		< 0.06
		Blank 2		< 0.06
C3		Deionized water 1		< 0.06
		Deionized water 2		< 0.06
		Deionized water 3		< 0.06
		Blank		< 0.06
C4		Deionized water 1		< 0.06
		Deionized water 2		0.41
		Deionized water 3		0.60
		Blank		< 0.06
C5		Deionized water 1		0.84
		Deionized water 2		0.90
		Blank		0.10
C6		Deionized water 1		0.19
		Deionized water 2		0.26
		Deionized water 3		0.33
		Blank		0.16
		Precision, laboratory duplicates		
C1	6	A	7.87	605
	6	B	7.52	578
Average			7.70	592
Relative % Diff.			5	
C1	12	A	0.58	12.9
	12	B	0.52	11.6
Average			0.55	12.2
Relative % Diff.			11	
C1	17	A	0.38	1.58
	17	B	0.45	1.87
Average			0.42	1.74
Relative % Diff.			17	
C1	20	A	0.66	2.46
	20	B	0.67	2.50
Average			0.67	2.50
Relative % Diff.			1	
C2	6	A	2.06	22.6
	6	B	2.93	32.2
Average			2.50	27.5
Relative % Diff.			35	
C2	16	A	2.95	13.8
	16	B	3.80	17.8
Average			3.37	15.8
Relative % Diff.			25	

Appendix 2. Analytical quality-assurance and quality-control data for soil samples collected in 2006 at six sites in the Lost Creek Designated Ground Water Basin, Colorado.—Continued

[µg/g, micrograms of chloride per gram of sediment; mg/L, milligrams of chloride per liter of water; Relative % Diff., the difference between duplicate or replicate analyses divided by the average of the analyses and expressed as percent; Grand Avg. Precision, the average of Relative % Diff. for all duplicate samples]

Site[1]	Depth (ft)	Quality-control sample	Chloride concentration (µg/g)	Chloride concentration (mg/L)
Precision, laboratory duplicates—Continued				
C3	6	A	1.66	9.33
	6	B	2.04	11.5
Average			1.85	10.4
Relative % Diff.			20	
C3	14	A	211	1,160
	14	B	215	1,180
Average			213	1,170
Relative % Diff.			2	
C4	6	A	1.36	11.1
	6	B	2.64	21.5
Average			2.00	16.3
Relative % Diff.			64	
C4	18	A	5.76	29.5
	18	B	3.01	15.4
Average			4.38	22.5
Relative % Diff.			63	
C5	8	A	27.1	172
	8	B	10.9	69.0
Average			19.0	120
Relative % Diff.			85	
C5	18	A	2.64	10.9
	18	B	1.87	7.70
Average			2.26	9.30
Relative % Diff.			34	
C6	8	A	2.13	12.3
	8	B	1.28	7.40
Average			1.71	9.88
Relative % Diff.			50	
C6	16	A	2.37	11.1
	16	B	2.97	13.9
Average			2.67	12.5
Relative % Diff.			23	
Grand Avg. Precision			31	
Precision, field replicates				
C1	20	A	0.66	2.46
	20	B	0.61	2.28
Average			0.63	2.35
Relative % Diff.			9	

[1]Site for deionized water and blank samples indicates site of field samples for which deionized water and blank samples are associated. All deionized water and blank samples are laboratory procedural quality-control samples. Deionized water or a blank sample generally was analyzed after about every third field sample.

Appendix 3.   Chloride in wet and dry deposition at the National Atmospheric Deposition Program Pawnee site (Site ID CO22), Colorado.

[Date in month/day/year; kg/ha/yr, kilogram per hectare per year; cm/yr, centimeters per year; mg/L, milligrams per liter]

Wet deposition[1]				Dry deposition[2]		
Period of measurement		Chloride deposition rate (kg/ha/yr)	Precipitation rate (cm/yr)	Period of measurement		Chloride deposition rate (kg/ha/yr)
Start date	End date			Start date	End date	
5/22/1979	1/1/1980	0.49	33.09	10/2/1979	11/6/1979	0.05
1/1/1980	12/30/1980	0.63	32.99	11/6/1979	1/1/1980	0.07
12/30/1980	12/29/1981	0.51	34.38	3/4/1980	4/1/1980	0.31
12/29/1981	1/4/1983	0.32	41.41	4/1/1980	6/3/1980	0.17
1/4/1983	1/3/1984	0.47	37.28	10/7/1980	12/2/1980	0.12
1/3/1984	1/2/1985	0.64	41.48	12/2/1980	1/27/1981	0.06
1/2/1985	12/31/1985	0.35	29.35	1/27/1981	3/24/1981	0.03
12/31/1985	12/30/1986	0.23	24.52	7/21/1981	9/8/1981	0.13
12/30/1986	12/29/1987	0.36	31.19	9/8/1981	11/3/1981	0.06
12/29/1987	1/3/1989	0.28	31.42	11/3/1981	12/30/1981	0.05
1/3/1989	1/2/1990	0.29	28.91	12/30/1981	2/23/1982	0.03
1/2/1990	1/2/1991	0.35	27.97	2/23/1982	4/20/1982	0.04
1/2/1991	12/31/1991	0.31	31.23	4/20/1982	6/15/1982	0.23
12/31/1991	12/29/1992	0.25	34.36	10/5/1982	12/1/1982	0.04
12/29/1992	1/4/1994	0.37	36.88	12/1/1982	1/25/1983	0.04
1/4/1994	1/3/1995	0.17	24.14	1/25/1983	3/23/1983	0.05
1/3/1995	1/2/1996	0.3	40.66	9/6/1983	11/1/1983	0.09
1/2/1996	12/30/1996	0.41	37.37	11/1/1983	12/27/1983	0.04
12/30/1996	12/30/1997	0.34	51.88	12/27/1983	2/14/1984	0.06
12/30/1997	12/29/1998	0.21	28.62	10/2/1984	11/27/1984	0.04
12/29/1998	12/28/1999	0.27	47.88	2/12/1985	3/19/1985	0.03
12/28/1999	1/2/2001	0.16	21.92	3/19/1985	5/14/1985	0.12
1/2/2001	1/1/2002	0.22	29.47	7/9/1985	9/3/1985	0.04
1/1/2002	12/31/2002	0.12	17.67	9/3/1985	10/29/1985	0.04
12/31/2002	12/30/2003	0.2	30.57	10/29/1985	12/24/1985	0.03
12/30/2003	12/28/2004	0.19	26.18	12/24/1985	2/18/1986	0.03
Average		**0.32**	**32.80**	2/18/1986	4/15/1986	0.05
				4/15/1986	6/10/1986	0.15
				11/25/1986	1/20/1987	0.06
				1/20/1987	3/17/1987	0.05
				3/17/1987	5/12/1987	0.06
				7/7/1987	9/1/1987	0.13
				9/3/1987	10/27/1987	0.08
				10/27/1987	12/22/1987	0.07
				12/22/1987	2/16/1988	0.04
				2/16/1988	4/12/1988	0.45
				4/12/1988	6/7/1988	0.42
				6/7/1988	8/23/1988	0.32
				8/23/1988	9/27/1988	0.12
				9/27/1988	11/22/1988	0.05
				11/22/1988	1/3/1989	0.04
				1/3/1989	1/17/1989	0.03
				1/17/1989	3/14/1989	0.03
				5/9/1989	8/8/1989	0.16
				8/8/1989	8/29/1989	0.06
				8/29/1989	10/24/1989	0.04
				10/24/1989	12/19/1989	0.04
				12/19/1989	2/13/1990	0.03
				2/13/1990	4/9/1990	0.04
				4/9/1990	6/5/1990	0.09
				6/5/1990	7/31/1990	0.10
				Average		**0.09**
[3]**Average effective chloride concentration of precipitation, in milligrams per liter**						**0.13**

[1]Wet-deposition data from National Atmospheric Deposition Program (2005).

[2]Dry-depostion data from Robert Larson, National Atmospheric Deposition Program (written commun., 2006).

[3]Average effective chloride concentration of precipitation calculated as the sum of average wet and dry deposition rates, divided by the average precipitation rate, converted to units of milligrams per liter.

Appendix 4.   Net irrigation, precipitation, crop evapotranspiration, and lysimeter-drainage data for four sites in the Lost Creek Designated Ground Water Basin, Colorado, 2007–2008

Site L1

Latitude/longitude: 40°03'18.8"/104°24'50.4", North American Datum of 1983
Irrigation method: center-pivot sprinkler
Soil type: loam
Crop type: alfalfa
[--, no data or not reported]

	2007					2008			
Date	Net irrigation[1] (inches)	Precipitation[2] (inches)	Crop evapo-transpiration[3] (inches)	Lysimeter drainage (inches)	Date	Net irrigation[1] (inches)	Precipitation[2] (inches)	Crop evapo-transpiration[3] (inches)	Lysimeter drainage (inches)
06/03/2007	0.75	0.00	0.24	0.00	04/08/2008	0.50	0.00	0.05	0.00
06/04/2007	0.00	0.00	0.24	0.00	04/09/2008	0.00	0.00	0.04	0.00
06/05/2007	0.60	0.00	0.33	0.00	04/10/2008	0.00	0.02	0.01	0.00
06/06/2007	0.00	0.00	0.52	0.00	04/11/2008	0.00	0.16	0.06	0.00
06/07/2007	0.00	0.00	0.35	0.00	04/12/2008	0.00	0.10	0.07	0.00
06/08/2007	0.00	0.00	0.34	0.00	04/13/2008	0.00	0.12	0.08	0.00
06/09/2007	0.00	0.00	0.35	0.00	04/14/2008	0.00	0.52	0.14	0.00
06/10/2007	0.65	0.00	0.39	0.00	04/15/2008	0.00	1.00	0.24	0.00
06/11/2007	0.65	0.11	0.44	0.00	04/16/2008	0.00	0.00	0.11	0.00
06/12/2007	0.00	0.05	0.11	0.00	04/17/2008	0.00	0.06	0.11	0.00
06/13/2007	0.65	0.00	0.25	0.00	04/18/2008	0.00	0.03	0.17	0.00
06/14/2007	0.75	0.00	0.31	0.00	04/19/2008	0.65	0.19	0.31	0.00
06/15/2007	0.00	0.00	0.37	0.13	04/20/2008	0.00	0.24	0.38	0.00
06/16/2007	0.75	0.00	0.45	0.00	04/21/2008	0.65	0.21	0.23	0.00
06/17/2007	0.00	0.01	0.52	0.00	04/22/2008	0.00	0.18	0.31	0.00
06/18/2007	0.00	0.00	0.39	0.00	04/23/2008	0.00	0.00	0.33	0.00
06/19/2007	0.00	0.00	0.37	0.00	04/24/2008	0.00	0.00	0.37	0.00
06/20/2007	0.75	0.00	0.46	0.00	04/25/2008	0.00	0.00	0.21	0.00
06/21/2007	0.00	0.00	0.51	0.00	04/26/2008	0.00	0.00	0.19	0.00
06/22/2007	0.75	0.57	0.3	0.00	04/27/2008	0.00	0.00	0.29	0.00
06/23/2007	0.00	0.00	0.36	0.00	04/28/2008	0.75	0.00	0.24	0.00
06/24/2007	0.75	0.00	0.49	0.00	04/29/2008	0.00	0.00	0.32	0.00
06/25/2007	0.00	0.00	0.52	0.00	04/30/2008	0.75	0.01	0.48	0.00
06/26/2007	0.00	0.00	0.25	0.00	05/01/2008	0.00	0.00	0.09	0.00
06/27/2007	0.00	0.00	First cut[4]	0.00	05/02/2008	0.00	0.00	0.12	0.00
06/28/2007	0.00	0.00	--	0.00	05/03/2008	0.00	0.00	0.19	0.00
06/29/2007	0.00	0.00	--	0.00	05/04/2008	0.00	0.00	0.28	0.00
06/30/2007	0.00	0.00	--	0.00	05/05/2008	0.00	0.00	0.27	0.00
07/01/2007	0.00	0.06	--	0.00	05/06/2008	0.75	0.01	0.34	0.00
07/02/2007	0.00	0.00	0.16	0.00	05/07/2008	0.00	0.02	0.15	0.00
07/03/2007	0.00	0.00	0.16	0.00	05/08/2008	0.00	0.00	0.24	0.00
07/04/2007	0.00	0.00	0.12	0.00	05/09/2008	0.00	0.26	0.21	0.00
07/05/2007	0.00	0.00	0.15	0.00	05/10/2008	0.00	0.00	0.13	0.00
07/06/2007	0.00	0.00	0.21	0.00	05/11/2008	0.00	0.01	0.2	0.00
07/07/2007	0.00	0.00	0.26	0.00	05/12/2008	0.75	0.05	0.38	0.00
07/08/2007	0.75	0.28	0.16	0.00	05/13/2008	0.00	0.00	0.11	0.00
07/09/2007	0.00	0.00	0.22	0.00	05/14/2008	0.00	0.01	0.21	0.00
07/10/2007	0.00	0.00	0.21	0.00	05/15/2008	0.00	0.00	0.15	0.00
07/11/2007	0.75	0.07	0.29	0.00	05/16/2008	0.75	0.00	0.24	0.00
07/12/2007	0.00	0.37	0.18	0.09	05/17/2008	0.00	0.2	0.32	0.00
07/13/2007	0.00	0.00	0.24	0.00	05/18/2008	0.00	0.3	0.36	0.00
07/14/2007	0.75	0.00	0.29	0.12	05/19/2008	0.40	0.1	0.27	0.00
07/15/2007	0.00	0.00	0.34	0.12	05/20/2008	0.50	0.1	0.21	0.00
07/16/2007	0.75	0.00	0.36	0.00	05/21/2008	0.40	0.0	0.55	0.00
07/17/2007	0.00	0.00	0.43	0.00	05/22/2008	0.40	0.0	0.45	0.00
07/18/2007	0.75	0.00	0.33	0.00	05/23/2008	0.50	0.0	0.32	0.00

Appendix 4. Net irrigation, precipitation, crop evapotranspiration, and lysimeter-drainage data for four sites in the Lost Creek Designated Ground Water Basin, Colorado, 2007–2008.—Continued

Site L1

Latitude/longitude: 40°03'18.8"/104°24'50.4", North American Datum of 1983
Irrigation method: center-pivot sprinkler
Soil type: loam
Crop type: alfalfa
[--, no data or not reported]

	2007					2008			
Date	Net irrigation[1] (inches)	Precipitation[2] (inches)	Crop evapo-transpiration[3] (inches)	Lysimeter drainage (inches)	Date	Net irrigation[1] (inches)	Precipitation[2] (inches)	Crop evapo-transpiration[3] (inches)	Lysimeter drainage (inches)
07/19/2007	0.00	0.00	0.25	0.00	05/24/2008	0.00	0.0	0.14	0.00
07/20/2007	0.75	0.00	0.39	0.00	05/25/2008	0.00	0.0	0.26	0.00
07/21/2007	0.00	0.11	0.43	0.00	05/26/2008	0.00	0.0	0.12	0.00
07/22/2007	0.75	0.00	0.4	0.00	05/27/2008	0.00	0.0	0.14	0.00
07/23/2007	0.00	0.00	0.34	0.00	05/28/2008	0.40	0.0	0.3	0.00
07/24/2007	0.75	0.00	0.38	0.12	05/29/2008	0.40	0.0	0.29	0.00
07/25/2007	0.00	0.00	0.46	0.00	05/30/2008	0.00	0.0	0.19	0.00
07/26/2007	0.75	0.00	0.28	0.08	05/31/2008	0.00	0.0	0.27	0.00
07/27/2007	0.00	1.37	0.23	0.00	06/01/2008	0.00	0.0	0.3	0.00
07/28/2007	0.00	0.10	0.17	0.00	06/02/2008	0.00	0.0	0.3	0.00
07/29/2007	0.00	0.00	Second cut[4]	0.00	06/03/2008	0.00	0.0	0.21	0.00
07/30/2007	0.00	0.00	--	0.00	06/04/2008	0.00	0.0	0.23	0.00
07/31/2007	0.00	0.00	--	0.00	06/05/2008	0.00	0.0	0.11	0.00
08/01/2007	0.00	0.04	--	0.00	06/06/2008	0.00	0.0	0.23	0.00
08/02/2007	0.00	0.21	--	0.00	06/07/2008	0.00	0.0	0.21	0.00
08/03/2007	0.00	0.47	0.09	0.00	06/08/2008	0.00	0.0	0.22	0.00
08/04/2007	0.00	0.00	0.1	0.00	06/09/2008	0.00	0.0	0.21	0.00
08/05/2007	0.00	0.09	0.1	0.00	06/10/2008	0.00	0.0	0.42	0.00
08/06/2007	0.00	0.19	0.06	0.00	06/11/2008	0.00	0.0	0.3	0.00
08/07/2007	0.00	0.03	0.08	0.09	06/12/2008	0.00	0.0	0.29	0.00
08/08/2007	0.00	0.01	0.11	0.01	06/13/2008	0.50	0.0	0.15	0.00
08/09/2007	0.00	0.1	0.15	0.03	06/14/2008	0.55	0.0	First cut[4]	0.00
08/10/2007	0.00	0.0	0.14	0.00	06/15/2008	0.55	0.0	--	0.00
08/11/2007	0.00	0.0	0.17	0.00	06/16/2008	0.40	0.0	--	0.00
08/12/2007	0.00	0.0	0.18	0.00	06/17/2008	0.55	0.0	--	0.00
08/13/2007	0.00	0.0	0.21	0.00	06/18/2008	0.00	0.0	--	0.00
08/14/2007	0.00	0.0	0.22	0.00	06/19/2008	0.30	0.0	0.07	0.00
08/15/2007	0.00	0.0	0.16	0.00	06/20/2008	0.50	0.0	0.06	0.00
08/16/2007	0.00	0.0	0.2	0.00	06/21/2008	0.00	0.0	0.06	0.00
08/17/2007	0.00	0.0	0.28	0.00	06/22/2008	0.55	0.0	0.09	0.00
08/18/2007	0.00	0.0	0.24	0.00	06/23/2008	0.55	0.0	0.09	0.00
08/19/2007	0.00	0.0	0.24	0.00	06/24/2008	0.50	0.0	0.09	0.00
08/20/2007	0.00	0.0	0.3	0.00	06/25/2008	0.00	0.0	0.1	0.00
08/21/2007	0.00	0.0	0.31	0.00	06/26/2008	0.50	0.0	0.1	0.00
08/22/2007	0.00	0.0	0.2	0.00	06/27/2008	0.50	0.0	0.11	0.00
08/23/2007	0.00	0.0	0.14	0.00	06/28/2008	0.50	0.0	0.12	0.00
08/24/2007	0.00	0.3	0.25	0.00	06/29/2008	0.00	0.0	0.09	0.00
08/25/2007	0.00	0.0	0.23	0.00	06/30/2008	0.00	0.0	0.13	0.00
08/26/2007	0.00	0.0	0.31	0.00	07/01/2008	0.50	0.0	0.15	0.00
08/27/2007	0.75	0.1	0.28	0.00	07/02/2008	0.45	0.0	0.14	0.00
08/28/2007	0.00	0.0	0.23	0.00	07/03/2008	0.65	0.0	0.05	0.00
08/29/2007	0.75	0.0	0.18	0.00	07/04/2008	0.00	0.0	0.12	0.00
08/30/2007	0.00	0.0	0.32	0.00	07/05/2008	0.40	0.0	0.2	0.00
08/31/2007	0.00	0.0	0.34	0.00	07/06/2008	0.40	0.0	0.12	0.00
09/01/2007	0.75	0.0	0.26	0.08	07/07/2008	0.60	0.0	0.1	0.00
09/02/2007	0.00	0.0	0.3	0.01	07/08/2008	0.00	0.0	0.12	0.00

Appendix 4. Net irrigation, precipitation, crop evapotranspiration, and lysimeter-drainage data for four sites in the Lost Creek Designated Ground Water Basin, Colorado, 2007–2008.—Continued

Site L1

Latitude/longitude: 40°03'18.8"/104°24'50.4", North American Datum of 1983
Irrigation method: center-pivot sprinkler
Soil type: loam
Crop type: alfalfa
[--, no data or not reported]

	2007					2008			
Date	Net irrigation[1] (inches)	Precipitation[2] (inches)	Crop evapo-transpiration[3] (inches)	Lysimeter drainage (inches)	Date	Net irrigation[1] (inches)	Precipitation[2] (inches)	Crop evapo-transpiration[3] (inches)	Lysimeter drainage (inches)
09/03/2007	0.75	0.0	0.29	0.08	07/09/2008	0.00	0.0	0.26	0.00
09/04/2007	0.00	0.0	0.3	0.00	07/10/2008	0.00	0.0	0.22	0.00
09/05/2007	0.00	0.1	0.35	0.00	07/11/2008	0.00	0.0	0.43	0.00
09/06/2007	0.70	0.0	0.24	0.00	07/12/2008	0.00	0.0	0.18	0.00
09/07/2007	0.00	0.0	0.26	0.00	07/13/2008	0.00	0.0	0.31	0.00
09/08/2007	0.00	0.0	0.36	0.00	07/14/2008	0.00	0.0	0.28	0.00
09/09/2007	0.00	0.0	0.18	0.00	07/15/2008	0.00	0.0	0.31	0.00
09/10/2007	0.00	0.0	0.18	0.00	07/16/2008	0.00	0.0	0.34	0.00
09/11/2007	0.00	0.0	0.25	0.00	07/17/2008	0.00	0.0	0.15	0.00
09/12/2007	0.65	0.0	0.3	0.00	07/18/2008	0.00	0.0	0.15	0.00
09/13/2007	0.00	0.0	0.22	0.00	07/19/2008	0.00	0.0	0.17	0.00
09/14/2007	0.00	0.0	0.25	0.00	07/20/2008	0.00	0.0	0.31	0.00
09/15/2007	0.00	0.0	Third cut[4]	0.00	07/21/2008	0.70	0.0	0.17	0.00
09/16/2007	0.00	0.0	--	0.00	07/22/2008	0.00	0.0	0.18	0.00
09/17/2007	0.00	0.1	--	0.00	07/23/2008	0.75	0.0	0.23	0.00
09/18/2007	0.00	0.0	--	0.00	07/24/2008	0.00	0.0	0.15	0.00
09/19/2007	0.00	0.0	--	0.00	07/25/2008	0.80	0.0	0.16	0.00
09/20/2007	0.00	0.0	0.11	0.00	07/26/2008	0.00	0.0	0.11	0.00
09/21/2007	0.00	0.0	0.12	0.00	07/27/2008	0.80	0.0	0.16	0.00
09/22/2007	0.00	0.0	0.16	0.00	07/28/2008	0.00	0.0	0.13	0.00
09/23/2007	0.00	0.0	0.16	0.00	07/29/2008	0.80	0.0	0.12	0.00
09/24/2007	0.00	0.1	0.06	0.00	07/30/2008	0.80	0.0	0.28	0.00
09/25/2007	0.00	0.0	0.08	0.00	07/31/2008	0.00	0.0	0.21	0.00
09/26/2007	0.00	0.0	0.09	0.00	08/01/2008	0.00	0.0	0.16	0.00
09/27/2007	0.00	0.0	0.13	0.00	08/02/2008	0.80	0.0	0.22	0.00
09/28/2007	0.00	0.00	0.23	0.00	08/03/2008	0.80	0.0	0.22	0.12
09/29/2007	0.50	0.00	0.3	0.00	08/04/2008	0.00	0.0	0.17	0.15
09/30/2007	0.00	0.25	0.18	0.00	08/05/2008	0.80	0.0	0.11	0.03
10/01/2007	0.00	0.00	0.17	0.00	08/06/2008	0.00	0.0	0.14	0.21
10/02/2007	0.00	0.00	0.28	0.00	08/07/2008	0.00	0.0	0.06	0.28
10/03/2007	0.00	0.00	0.21	0.00	08/08/2008	0.00	0.0	0.11	0.08
10/04/2007	0.00	0.00	0.28	0.00	08/09/2008	0.00	0.2	0.06	0.12
10/05/2007	0.75	0.00	0.27	0.00	08/10/2008	0.00	0.2	0.06	0.43
10/06/2007	0.00	0.00	0.59	0.00	08/11/2008	0.00	0.2	0.09	0.03
10/07/2007	0.00	0.00	0.16	0.00	08/12/2008	0.00	0.0	0.1	0.00
10/08/2007	0.00	0.00	Fourth cut[4]	0.00	08/13/2008	0.00	0.0	0.16	0.11
10/09/2007	0.00	0.00	--	0.00	08/14/2008	0.00	0.0	0.1	0.17
10/10/2007	0.00	0.00	--	0.00	08/15/2008	0.00	0.0	0.07	0.00
10/11/2007	0.00	0.00	--	0.00	08/16/2008	0.00	0.0	0.08	0.00
10/12/2007	0.00	0.00	--	0.00	08/17/2008	0.00	0.0	0.25	0.00
10/13/2007	0.00	0.05	0.01	0.00	08/18/2008	0.00	0.0	0.05	0.00
10/14/2007	0.00	0.4	0.01	0.00	08/19/2008	0.00	0.0	0.13	0.04
10/15/2007	0.00	0.01	0.09	0.00	08/20/2008	0.00	0.0	0.15	0.04
10/16/2007	0.00	0.00	0.1	0.00	08/21/2008	0.00	0.0	0.14	0.00
10/17/2007	0.00	0.00	0.14	0.00	08/22/2008	0.00	0.0	0.13	0.00
10/18/2007	0.00	0.00	0.23	0.00	08/23/2008	0.00	0.0	0.11	0.00

Appendix 4.   Net irrigation, precipitation, crop evapotranspiration, and lysimeter-drainage data for four sites in the Lost Creek Designated Ground Water Basin, Colorado, 2007–2008.—Continued

Site L1

Latitude/longitude: 40°03'18.8"/104°24'50.4", North American Datum of 1983
Irrigation method: center-pivot sprinkler
Soil type: loam
Crop type: alfalfa
[--, no data or not reported]

	2007					2008			
Date	**Net irrigation[1] (inches)**	**Precipitation[2] (inches)**	**Crop evapo-transpiration[3] (inches)**	**Lysimeter drainage (inches)**	**Date**	**Net irrigation[1] (inches)**	**Precipitation[2] (inches)**	**Crop evapo-transpiration[3] (inches)**	**Lysimeter drainage (inches)**
10/19/2007	0.00	0.00	0.2	0.00	08/24/2008	0.00	0.0	0.12	0.00
10/20/2007	0.00	0.05	0.29	0.00	08/25/2008	0.00	0.0	Second cut[4]	0.00
Total	**19.4**	**5.7**	**30.5**	**1.0**	08/26/2008	0.00	0.0	--	0.00
					08/27/2008	0.00	0.0	--	0.00
					08/28/2008	0.00	0.0	--	0.00
					08/29/2008	0.00	0.0	--	0.00
					08/30/2008	0.00	0.0	0.08	0.00
					08/31/2008	0.00	0.0	0.07	0.00
					09/01/2008	0.00	0.0	0.06	0.00
					09/02/2008	0.00	0.0	0.09	0.00
					09/03/2008	0.00	0.0	0.06	0.00
					09/04/2008	0.00	0.0	0.04	0.00
					09/05/2008	0.00	0.0	0.07	0.00
					09/06/2008	0.00	0.0	0.03	0.00
					09/07/2008	0.00	0.0	0.07	0.00
					09/08/2008	0.00	0.0	0.06	0.00
					09/09/2008	0.75	0.0	0.05	0.00
					09/10/2008	0.00	0.0	0.05	0.00
					09/11/2008	0.75	0.0	0.05	0.00
					09/12/2008	0.00	0.0	0.05	0.00
					09/13/2008	0.00	0.1	0.09	0.00
					09/14/2008	0.00	0.0	0.03	0.00
					09/15/2008	0.00	0.5	0.05	0.00
					09/16/2008	0.00	0.0	0.06	0.00
					09/17/2008	0.00	0.0	0.06	0.00
					Total	**26.6**	**5.0**	**26.7**	**1.8**

[1]Net irrigation based on farmer's records.

[2]Precipitation measured at CoAgMet Fort Morgan station (fig. 2).

[3]Crop evapotranspiration estimated by using the evapotranspiration calculator provided by the Colorado Agricultural Meteorological Network at *http //ccc.atmos.colostate.edu/cgi-bin/extended_etr_form.pl*. Crop evapotranspiration was calculated using the Penman-Monteith combination equation (Jensen and others, 1990) with data from the Colorado Agricultural Meteorological Network Fort Morgan station.

[4]Alfalfa crops were cut multiple times during the period of analysis. Alfalfa crops were assumed to become reestablished 5 days after each cut for the purpose of estimating evapotranspiration.

Appendix 4.   Net irrigation, precipitation, crop evapotranspiration, and lysimeter-drainage data for four sites in the Lost Creek Designated Ground Water Basin, Colorado, 2007–2008.—Continued

Site L2

Latitude/longitude: 40°03'37.6"/104°25'25.0", North American Datum of 1983
Irrigation method: flood furrow
Soil type: loam
Crop type: wheat

| | 2007 | | | | | 2008 | | | |
Date	Net irrigation[1] (inches)	Precipitation[2] (inches)	Crop evapo-transpiration[3] (inches)	Lysimeter drainage (inches)	Date	Net irrigation[1] (inches)	Precipitation[2] (inches)	Crop evapo-transpiration[3] (inches)	Lysimeter drainage (inches)
05/19/2007	0.22	0.00	0.28	0.00					
05/20/2007	0.00	0.00	0.33	0.00	No data[4]				
05/21/2007	0.00	0.00	0.28	0.00					
05/22/2007	0.00	0.34	0.23	0.00					
05/23/2007	0.00	0.00	0.18	0.00					
05/24/2007	0.00	0.00	0.25	0.00					
05/25/2007	0.00	0.00	0.33	0.00					
05/26/2007	0.00	0.00	0.28	0.00					
05/27/2007	0.00	0.00	0.34	0.00					
05/28/2007	0.00	0.47	0.37	0.00					
05/29/2007	0.00	0.48	0.23	0.00					
05/30/2007	0.22	0.00	0.21	0.00					
05/31/2007	0.00	0.00	0.29	0.04					
06/01/2007	0.00	0.00	0.18	0.00					
06/02/2007	0.00	0.00	0.25	0.00					
06/03/2007	0.00	0.00	0.24	0.00					
06/04/2007	0.00	0.00	0.24	0.00					
06/05/2007	0.00	0.00	0.33	0.00					
06/06/2007	0.00	0.00	0.52	0.00					
06/07/2007	0.00	0.00	0.35	0.00					
06/08/2007	0.00	0.00	0.34	0.00					
06/09/2007	0.00	0.00	0.35	0.00					
06/10/2007	0.00	0.00	0.39	0.00					
06/11/2007	0.00	0.00	0.44	0.00					
06/12/2007	0.00	0.16	0.11	0.00					
06/13/2007	0.00	0.00	0.24	0.03					
06/14/2007	0.00	0.00	0.3	0.00					
06/15/2007	0.00	0.00	0.35	0.04					
Total	**0.5**	**1.5**	**8.2**	**0.1**					

[1]Net irrigation calculated as the total volume of water pumped to field minus estimated runoff (10 percent of pumped water), divided by the number of irrigated acres (32). Pumping data were provided by the farmer.

[2]Precipitation measured at CoAgMet Fort Morgan station (fig. 2).

[3]Crop evapotranspiration estimated by using the evapotranspiration calculator provided by the Colorado Agricultural Meteorological Network at *http //ccc.atmos.colostate.edu/cgi-bin/extended_etr_form.pl.* Crop evapotranspiration was calculated using the Penman-Monteith combination equation (Jensen and others, 1990) with data from the Colorado Agricultural Meteorological Network Fort Morgan station.

[4]No data are reported for 2008 because furrows overlying lysimeter were not used in 2008.

Appendix 4. Net irrigation, precipitation, crop evapotranspiration, and lysimeter-drainage data for four sites in the Lost Creek Designated Ground Water Basin, Colorado, 2007–2008.—Continued

Site L3

Latitude/longitude: 40°07'06.9"/104°24'51.7", North American Datum of 1983
Irrigation method: flood furrow
Soil type: loam
Crop type: corn

| | 2007 | | | | | 2008 | | | |
Date	Net irrigation[1] (inches)	Precipitation[2] (inches)	Crop evapo- transpiration[3] (inches)	Lysimeter drainage (inches)	Date	Net irrigation[1] (inches)	Precipitation[2] (inches)	Crop evapo- transpiration[3] (inches)	Lysimeter drainage (inches)
06/22/2007	0.93	0.57	0.23	0.00					
06/23/2007	0.93	0.00	0.28	0.00	No data[4]				
06/24/2007	0.93	0.00	0.39	0.04					
06/25/2007	0.93	0.00	0.42	0.00					
06/26/2007	0.00	0.00	0.21	0.07					
06/27/2007	0.00	0.00	0.23	0.00					
06/28/2007	0.00	0.00	0.29	0.00					
06/29/2007	0.00	0.00	0.36	0.00					
06/30/2007	0.00	0.06	0.38	0.00					
07/01/2007	0.00	0.00	0.44	0.00					
07/02/2007	0.00	0.00	0.43	0.00					
07/03/2007	0.00	0.00	0.41	0.00					
07/04/2007	0.00	0.00	0.3	0.00					
07/05/2007	0.00	0.00	0.33	0.00					
07/06/2007	0.00	0.00	0.42	0.00					
07/07/2007	0.93	0.00	0.44	0.00					
07/08/2007	0.93	0.28	0.26	0.00					
07/09/2007	0.93	0.00	0.31	0.00					
07/10/2007	0.93	0.00	0.28	0.00					
07/11/2007	0.00	0.07	0.35	0.12					
07/12/2007	0.00	0.37	0.21	0.00					
07/13/2007	0.00	0.00	0.27	0.00					
07/14/2007	0.00	0.00	0.3	0.00					
07/15/2007	0.00	0.00	0.34	0.00					
07/16/2007	0.93	0.00	0.35	0.22					
07/17/2007	0.93	0.00	0.41	0.20					
07/18/2007	0.93	0.00	0.31	0.00					
07/19/2007	0.93	0.00	0.24	0.00					
07/20/2007	0.00	0.00	0.37	0.00					
07/21/2007	0.00	0.11	0.41	0.00					
07/22/2007	0.00	0.00	0.38	0.00					
07/23/2007	0.93	0.00	0.33	0.00					
07/24/2007	0.93	0.00	0.37	0.39					
07/25/2007	0.93	0.00	0.44	0.00					
07/26/2007	0.93	0.00	0.27	0.00					
07/27/2007	0.00	1.37	0.22	0.00					
07/28/2007	0.00	0.10	0.16	0.00					
07/29/2007	0.00	0.00	0.22	0.00					
07/30/2007	0.00	0.00	0.25	0.00					
07/31/2007	0.00	0.00	0.29	0.00					
08/01/2007	0.00	0.04	0.26	0.00					
08/02/2007	0.00	0.21	0.21	0.00					
08/03/2007	0.00	0.47	0.22	0.00					
08/04/2007	0.93	0.00	0.24	0.00					
08/05/2007	0.93	0.09	0.24	1.01					
08/06/2007	0.93	0.19	0.15	1.02					
08/07/2007	0.93	0.03	0.18	0.00					

Appendix 4. Net irrigation, precipitation, crop evapotranspiration, and lysimeter-drainage data for four sites in the Lost Creek Designated Ground Water Basin, Colorado, 2007–2008.—Continued

Site L3

Latitude/longitude: 40°07'06.9"/104°24'51.7", North American Datum of 1983
Irrigation method: flood furrow
Soil type: loam
Crop type: corn

	2007					2008			
Date	Net irrigation[1] (inches)	Precipitation[2] (inches)	Crop evapo-transpiration[3] (inches)	Lysimeter drainage (inches)	Date	Net irrigation[1] (inches)	Precipitation[2] (inches)	Crop evapo-transpiration[3] (inches)	Lysimeter drainage (inches)
08/08/2007	0.00	0.01	0.22	0.00					
08/09/2007	0.00	0.08	0.26	0.00					
08/10/2007	0.00	0.00	0.22	0.00					
08/11/2007	0.00	0.00	0.24	0.00					
08/12/2007	0.00	0.00	0.22	0.00					
08/13/2007	0.00	0.00	0.23	0.00					
08/14/2007	0.00	0.00	0.22	0.00					
08/15/2007	0.00	0.00	0.15	0.00					
08/16/2007	0.00	0.00	0.17	0.00					
08/17/2007	0.00	0.00	0.21	0.00					
08/18/2007	0.00	0.00	0.17	0.00					
08/19/2007	0.93	0.00	0.16	0.00					
08/20/2007	0.93	0.00	0.19	0.05					
08/21/2007	0.93	0.00	0.18	0.16					
08/22/2007	0.93	0.02	0.11	0.00					
08/23/2007	0.00	0.00	0.07	0.00					
08/24/2007	0.00	0.28	0.13	0.00					
08/25/2007	0.00	0.00	0.11	0.00					
08/26/2007	0.00	0.00	0.14	0.00					
08/27/2007	0.93	0.11	0.13	0.00					
08/28/2007	0.93	0.04	0.1	0.20					
08/29/2007	0.93	0.03	0.07	0.00					
08/30/2007	0.93	0.00	0.12	0.00					
08/31/2007	0.00	0.00	0.12	0.00					
09/01/2007	0.00	0.00	0.08	0.00					
09/02/2007	0.00	0.00	0.09	0.00					
09/03/2007	0.00	0.00	0.08	0.00					
09/04/2007	0.00	0.00	0.07	0.00					
09/05/2007	0.00	0.06	0.08	0.00					
09/06/2007	0.00	0.01	0.05	0.00					
09/07/2007	0.00	0.00	0.06	0.00					
09/08/2007	0.00	0.00	0.08	0.00					
09/09/2007	0.00	0.04	0.04	0.00					
09/10/2007	0.00	0.00	0.04	0.00					
09/11/2007	0.00	0.00	0.06	0.00					
09/12/2007	0.00	0.00	0.07	0.00					
09/13/2007	0.00	0.00	0.05	0.00					
09/14/2007	0.00	0.00	0.06	0.00					
Total	**26.0**	**4.6**	**19.3**	**3.5**					

[1]Net irrigation calculated as the total volume of water pumped to field minus estimated runoff (30 percent of pumped water), divided by the number of irrigated acres (64). Pumping data were provided by the farmer.

[2]Precipitation measured at CoAgMet Fort Morgan station (fig. 2).

[3]Crop evapotranspiration estimated by using the evapotranspiration calculator provided by the Colorado Agricultural Meteorological Network at *http //ccc.atmos.colostate.edu/cgi-bin/extended_etr_form.pl.* Crop evapotranspiration was calculated using the Penman-Monteith combination equation (Jensen and others, 1990) with data from the Colorado Agricultural Meteorological Network Fort Morgan station.

[4]No data are reported for 2008 because furrows overlying lysimeter were not used in 2008.

Appendix 4. Net irrigation, precipitation, crop evapotranspiration, and lysimeter-drainage data for four sites in the Lost Creek Designated Ground Water Basin, Colorado, 2007–2008.—Continued

Site L4

Latitude/longitude: 40°09′43.6″/104°24′46.9″, North American Datum of 1983
Irrigation method: center-pivot sprinkler
Soil type: sand
Crop type: 2007—corn; 2008—alfalfa
[--, no data or not reported]

	2007					2008			
Date	Net irrigation[1] (inches)	Precipitation[2] (inches)	Crop evapo-transpiration[3] (inches)	Lysimeter drainage (inches)	Date	Net irrigation[1] (inches)	Precipitation[2] (inches)	Crop evapo-transpiration[3] (inches)	Lysimeter drainage[4] (inches)
06/30/2007	0.4	0	0.33	0.00	05/08/2008	0.50	0.00	--	--
07/01/2007	0.4	0.06	0.39	0.00	05/09/2008	0.00	0.26	--	--
07/02/2007	0.4	0	0.39	0.00	05/10/2008	0.00	0.00	--	0.04
07/03/2007	0	0	0.37	0.00	05/11/2008	0.00	0.01	--	--
07/04/2007	0	0	0.27	0.00	05/12/2008	0.00	0.05	--	0.08
07/05/2007	0.26	0	0.3	0.00	05/13/2008	0.25	0.00	--	--
07/06/2007	0.4	0	0.38	0.00	05/14/2008	0.00	0.01	--	0.04
07/07/2007	0	0	0.41	0.00	05/15/2008	0.00	0.00	--	0.04
07/08/2007	0.4	0.28	0.24	0.00	05/16/2008	0.00	0.00	--	0.00
07/09/2007	0	0	0.29	0.00	05/17/2008	0.00	0.16	--	--
07/10/2007	0	0	0.27	0.00	05/18/2008	0.30	0.31	--	0.04
07/11/2007	0	0.07	0.34	0.00	05/19/2008	0.00	0.07	--	0.08
07/12/2007	0.4	0.37	0.2	0.04	05/20/2008	0.00	0.14	--	0.00
07/13/2007	0.26	0	0.26	0.00	05/21/2008	0.00	0.01	--	0.04
07/14/2007	0	0	0.3	0.00	05/22/2008	0.30	0.00	--	0.00
07/15/2007	0.4	0	0.34	0.00	05/23/2008	0.00	0.00	0.11	0.00
07/16/2007	0.4	0	0.35	0.00	05/24/2008	0.00	0.00	0.05	0.04
07/17/2007	0	0	0.41	0.00	05/25/2008	0.00	0.00	0.09	0.00
07/18/2007	0.4	0	0.31	0.00	05/26/2008	0.00	0.00	0.04	0.00
07/19/2007	0	0	0.24	0.00	05/27/2008	0.35	0.00	0.05	0.00
07/20/2007	0	0	0.37	0.00	05/28/2008	0.00	0.00	0.12	0.00
07/21/2007	0.4	0.11	0.41	0.00	05/29/2008	0.00	0.00	0.12	0.04
07/22/2007	0.26	0	0.38	0.00	05/30/2008	0.00	0.00	0.09	0.00
07/23/2007	0	0	0.33	0.04	05/31/2008	0.00	0.00	0.13	0.00
07/24/2007	0.4	0	0.37	0.04	06/01/2008	0.00	0.00	0.16	0.00
07/25/2007	0	0	0.44	0.00	06/02/2008	0.40	0.00	0.18	0.00
07/26/2007	0.26	0	0.27	0.00	06/03/2008	0.00	0.00	0.13	0.00
07/27/2007	0	1.37	0.22	0.00	06/04/2008	0.00	0.00	0.15	0.00
07/28/2007	0.4	0.1	0.16	0.00	06/05/2008	0.00	0.00	0.08	0.00
07/29/2007	0.26	0	0.23	0.00	06/06/2008	0.00	0.00	0.17	0.00
07/30/2007	0	0	0.26	0.00	06/07/2008	0.00	0.00	0.16	0.00
07/31/2007	0.4	0	0.31	0.00	06/08/2008	0.00	0.00	0.18	0.04
08/01/2007	0	0.04	0.28	0.00	06/09/2008	0.00	0.00	0.18	0.00
08/02/2007	0	0.21	0.23	0.04	06/10/2008	0.00	0.00	0.38	0.00
08/03/2007	0	0.47	0.24	0.12	06/11/2008	0.30	0.00	0.28	0.00
08/04/2007	0.26	0	0.26	0.00	06/12/2008	0.00	0.00	0.28	0.00
08/05/2007	0	0.09	0.26	0.00	06/13/2008	0.00	0.00	0.15	0.04
08/06/2007	0.4	0.19	0.17	0.00	06/14/2008	0.00	0.00	0.14	0.04
08/07/2007	0	0.03	0.2	0.00	06/15/2008	0.40	0.00	0.33	0.43
08/08/2007	0.26	0.01	0.26	0.00	06/16/2008	0.00	0.00	0.19	0.24
08/09/2007	0	0.08	0.3	0.70	06/17/2008	0.00	0.00	0.25	0.00
08/10/2007	0.4	0	0.26	0.00	06/18/2008	0.40	0.00	0.22	0.00
08/11/2007	0.24	0	0.29	0.00	06/19/2008	0.00	0.00	0.2	0.00
08/12/2007	0.4	0	0.27	0.00	06/20/2008	0.00	0.00	0.17	0.00
08/13/2007	0	0	0.28	0.00	06/21/2008	0.00	0.00	0.16	0.00

Appendix 4.   Net irrigation, precipitation, crop evapotranspiration, and lysimeter-drainage data for four sites in the Lost Creek Designated Ground Water Basin, Colorado, 2007–2008.—Continued

Site L4

Latitude/longitude: 40°09′43.6″/104°24′46.9″, North American Datum of 1983
Irrigation method: center-pivot sprinkler
Soil type: sand
Crop type: 2007—corn; 2008—alfalfa
[--, no data or not reported]

| | 2007 | | | | | 2008 | | | |
Date	Net irrigation[1] (inches)	Precipitation[2] (inches)	Crop evapo-transpiration[3] (inches)	Lysimeter drainage (inches)	Date	Net irrigation[1] (inches)	Precipitation[2] (inches)	Crop evapo-transpiration[3] (inches)	Lysimeter drainage[4] (inches)
08/14/2007	0.26	0	0.28	0.52	06/22/2008	0.00	0.00	First cut[5]	0.00
08/15/2007	0	0	0.18	0.47	06/23/2008	0.00	0.00	--	0.04
08/16/2007	0.4	0	0.21	0.00	06/24/2008	0.00	0.00	--	0.00
08/17/2007	0	0	0.27	0.00	06/25/2008	0.00	0.00	--	0.00
08/18/2007	0	0	0.22	0.00	06/26/2008	0.00	0.00	--	0.00
08/19/2007	0.26	0	0.21	0.00	06/27/2008	0.00	0.00	0.08	0.00
08/20/2007	0	0	0.25	0.12	06/28/2008	0.30	0.00	0.08	0.00
08/21/2007	0.40	0	0.24	0.00	06/29/2008	0.00	0.00	0.06	0.00
08/22/2007	0	0	0.15	0.00	06/30/2008	0.00	0.00	0.08	0.00
08/23/2007	0	0	0.1	0.00	07/01/2008	0.40	0.00	0.09	0.00
08/24/2007	0.4	0.28	0.18	0.00	07/02/2008	0.00	0.00	0.08	0.00
08/25/2007	0	0	0.16	0.00	07/03/2008	0.30	0.00	0.03	0.00
08/26/2007	0.26	0	0.21	0.00	07/04/2008	0.00	0.00	0.07	0.00
08/27/2007	0	0.11	0.19	0.00	07/05/2008	0.00	0.00	0.12	0.00
08/28/2007	0	0.04	0.15	0.00	07/06/2008	0.00	0.00	0.08	0.00
08/29/2007	0	0.03	0.11	0.00	07/07/2008	0.40	0.00	0.06	0.00
08/30/2007	0.4	0	0.2	0.00	07/08/2008	0.00	0.00	0.08	0.00
08/31/2007	0	0	0.2	0.00	07/09/2008	0.00	0.00	0.17	0.00
09/01/2007	0	0	0.15	0.01	07/10/2008	0.40	0.00	0.15	0.04
09/02/2007	0.4	0	0.16	0.01	07/11/2008	0.00	0.00	0.31	0.00
09/03/2007	0	0	0.16	0.00	07/12/2008	0.30	0.00	0.13	0.00
09/04/2007	0	0	0.15	0.03	07/13/2008	0.00	0.00	0.24	0.00
09/05/2007	0	0.06	0.17	0.03	07/14/2008	0.00	0.00	0.23	0.00
09/06/2007	0.4	0.01	0.11	0.04	07/15/2008	0.30	0.00	0.28	0.04
09/07/2007	0	0	0.11	0.04	07/16/2008	0.00	0.00	0.32	0.00
09/08/2007	0	0	0.14	0.04	07/17/2008	0.40	0.00	0.14	0.00
09/09/2007	0	0.04	0.07	0.04	07/18/2008	0.00	0.00	0.14	0.04
09/10/2007	0.4	0	0.06	0.04	07/19/2008	0.25	0.00	0.16	0.04
09/11/2007	0	0	0.09	0.04	07/20/2008	0.00	0.00	0.31	0.04
09/12/2007	0.4	0	0.09	0.03	07/21/2008	0.00	0.00	0.17	0.00
09/13/2007	0	0	0.06	0.02	07/22/2008	0.40	0.00	0.18	0.00
09/14/2007	0	0	0.07	0.04	07/23/2008	0.00	0.00	0.23	0.04
09/15/2007	0	0	0.08	0.03	07/24/2008	0.00	0.00	0.15	0.08
09/16/2007	0.4	0	0.06	0.01	07/25/2008	0.40	0.00	0.16	0.00
09/17/2007	0	0.06	0.03	0.04	07/26/2008	0.00	0.00	0.11	0.00
09/18/2007	0	0	0.06	0.03	07/27/2008	0.30	0.00	0.16	0.04
09/19/2007	0	0	0.08	0.01	07/28/2008	0.00	0.00	0.13	0.00
09/20/2007	0.25	0	0.07	0.04	07/29/2008	0.40	0.00	0.12	0.12
09/21/2007	0	0	0.07	0.04	07/30/2008	0.00	0.00	0.28	0.35
09/22/2007	0	0	0.1	0.02	07/31/2008	0.00	0.00	0.21	0.00
09/23/2007	0	0.04	0.08	0.02	08/01/2008	0.00	0.00	0.16	0.00
09/24/2007	0	0.07	0.03	0.04	08/02/2008	0.50	0.00	0.22	0.08
09/25/2007	0	0	0.04	0.00	08/03/2008	0.00	0.00	0.22	0.04
09/26/2007	0	0	0.04	0.04	08/04/2008	0.30	0.00	0.17	0.12
09/27/2007	0	0	0.05	0.02	08/05/2008	0.00	0.00	0.11	0.08

Appendix 4. Net irrigation, precipitation, crop evapotranspiration, and lysimeter-drainage data for four sites in the Lost Creek Designated Ground Water Basin, Colorado, 2007–2008.—Continued

Site L4

Latitude/longitude: 40°09′43.6″/104°24′46.9″, North American Datum of 1983
Irrigation method: center-pivot sprinkler
Soil type: sand
Crop type: 2007—corn; 2008—alfalfa
[--, no data or not reported]

	2007					2008			
Date	Net irrigation[1] (inches)	Precipitation[2] (inches)	Crop evapo-transpiration[3] (inches)	Lysimeter drainage (inches)	Date	Net irrigation[1] (inches)	Precipitation[2] (inches)	Crop evapo-transpiration[3] (inches)	Lysimeter drainage[4] (inches)
09/28/2007	0	0	0.09	0.00	08/06/2008	0.00	0.04	0.14	0.00
09/29/2007	0	0	0.1	0.01	08/07/2008	0.40	0.01	0.06	0.00
09/30/2007	0	0.25	0.05	0.04	08/08/2008	0.00	0.01	0.11	0.00
10/01/2007	0	0	0.05	0.00	08/09/2008	0.00	0.15	0.06	0.00
10/02/2007	0	0	0.07	0.04	08/10/2008	0.00	0.17	0.06	0.00
10/03/2007	0	0	0.05	0.02	08/11/2008	0.00	0.17	0.09	0.00
10/04/2007	0	0	0.07	0.02	08/12/2008	0.00	0.00	0.10	0.00
10/05/2007	0	0	0.06	0.02	08/13/2008	0.00	0.00	0.16	0.04
Total	**13.1**	**4.5**	**19.9**	**3.0**	08/14/2008	0.30	0.00	0.10	0.00
					08/15/2008	0.00	0.01	0.07	0.04
					08/16/2008	0.00	0.01	0.08	0.00
					08/17/2008	0.00	0.00	0.25	0.00
					08/18/2008	0.00	0.00	0.05	0.00
					08/19/2008	0.00	0.00	0.13	0.04
					08/20/2008	0.30	0.00	0.15	0.00
					08/21/2008	0.00	0.00	0.14	0.00
					08/22/2008	0.40	0.00	0.13	0.00
					08/23/2008	0.00	0.00	0.11	0.00
					08/24/2008	0.30	0.00	0.12	0.00
					08/25/2008	0.00	0.00	0.15	0.08
					08/26/2008	0.00	0.00	0.12	0.00
					08/27/2008	0.30	0.00	0.08	0.00
					08/28/2008	0.00	0.00	0.10	0.00
					08/29/2008	0.25	0.00	0.15	0.00
					08/30/2008	0.00	0.00	0.22	0.08
					08/31/2008	0.00	0.00	0.20	0.00
					09/01/2008	0.00	0.00	0.17	--
					09/02/2008	0.40	0.00	0.25	0.16
					09/03/2008	0.00	0.00	0.16	0.24
					09/04/2008	0.25	0.00	0.11	0.39
					09/05/2008	0.00	0.00	0.17	0.04
					09/06/2008	0.00	0.00	0.07	0.35
					09/07/2008	0.25	0.00	0.17	0.20
					09/08/2008	0.00	0.01	0.12	0.00

Appendix 4.   Net irrigation, precipitation, crop evapotranspiration, and lysimeter-drainage data for four sites in the Lost Creek Designated Ground Water Basin, Colorado, 2007–2008.—Continued

Site L4

Latitude/longitude: 40°09′43.6″/104°24′46.9″, North American Datum of 1983
Irrigation method: center-pivot sprinkler
Soil type: sand
Crop type: 2007—corn; 2008—alfalfa
[--, no data or not reported]

		2007					2008		
Date	Net irrigation[1] (inches)	Precipitation[2] (inches)	Crop evapo-transpiration[3] (inches)	Lysimeter drainage (inches)	Date	Net irrigation[1] (inches)	Precipitation[2] (inches)	Crop evapo-transpiration[3] (inches)	Lysimeter drainage[4] (inches)
					09/09/2008	0.25	0.00	0.12	0.04
					09/10/2008	0.00	0.00	0.10	0.00
					09/11/2008	0.00	0.00	0.09	0.00
					09/12/2008	0.40	0.02	0.09	0.00
					09/13/2008	0.00	0.05	0.16	0.00
					09/14/2008	0.00	0.00	Second cut[5]	0.00
					09/15/2008	0.00	0.49	--	0.00
					09/16/2008	0.00	0.02	--	0.08
					09/17/2008	0.00	0.00	--	0.00
					09/18/2008	0.00	0.00	--	0.04
					09/19/2008	0.00	0.00	0.04	0.00
					09/20/2008	0.00	0.02	0.04	0.00
					09/21/2008	0.30	0.00	0.09	0.04
					09/22/2008	0.00	0.00	0.08	0.00
					09/23/2008	0.25	0.00	0.03	0.00
					09/24/2008	0.00	0.00	0.04	0.00
					09/25/2008	0.00	0.00	0.04	0.04
					09/26/2008	0.00	0.00	0.08	0.00
					09/27/2008	0.00	0.00	0.12	0.08
					09/28/2008	0.30	0.00	0.16	0.00
					09/29/2008	0.00	0.00	0.13	0.00
					09/30/2008	0.00	0.00	0.15	0.00
					Total	**13.2**	**2.2**	**17.1**	**4.0**

[1]Net irrigation based on farmer's records.

[2]Precipitation measured at CoAgMet Fort Morgan station (fig. 2).

[3]Crop evapotranspiration estimated by using the evapotranspiration calculator provided by the Colorado Agricultural Meteorological Network at *http //ccc.atmos.colostate.edu/cgi-bin/extended_etr_form.pl*. Crop evapotranspiration was calculated using the Penman-Monteith combination equation (Jensen and others, 1990) with data from the Colorado Agricultural Meteorological Network Fort Morgan station. Crop evapotranspiration not reported before 05/17/2008 to account for lack of evapotranspiration by newly planted crop prior to becoming established. Crop was planted 05/03/2008.

[4]Lysimeter drainage reported as "--" represents unreasonably high values likely resulting from lysimeter malfunction or flushing of center-pivot sprinkler system over lysimeter location.

[5]Alfalfa crops were cut multiple times during the period of analysis. Alfalfa crops were assumed to become reestablished 5 days after each cut for the purpose of estimating evapotranspiration.

Appendix 5.   Permitted acres, commingled acres, estimated irrigated acres, and estimated average annual withdrawals from decreed irrigation wells with final permits in the Lost Creek Designated Ground Water Basin.

[acre-ft, acre-feet]

Permit number[1]	Number of permitted acres[1]	Permit numbers of commingled wells[1]	Number of commingled acres[1]	Estimated number of irrigated acres[2]	Estimated average annual withdrawal[3] (acre-ft)	Estimated average annual application[4] (acre-ft/acre)
10249FP	80		0	80	128	1.6
10477FP	40	4061FP, 12811FP, 12812FP, 12813FP	423	40	64	1.6
10717FP	128	31580FP, 31581FP	128	43	68	1.6
10869FP	293	10870FP, 31565FP	293	98	156	1.6
10870FP	293	10869FP, 31565FP	293	98	156	1.6
11041FP	160		0	160	256	1.6
11417FP	160		0	160	256	1.6
11708FP	160	31575FP, 5035FP	160	53	85	1.6
11981FP	80	4497FP	80	40	64	1.6
12123FP	320	12124FP	320	119	**203.4**	1.7
12124FP	320	12123FP	320	106	**181.2**	1.7
12172FP	160		0	160	256	1.6
12174FP	160		0	160	256	1.6
12177FP	160		0	160	256	1.6
12470FP	80	5036FP	80	40	64	1.6
12505FP	160		0	160	256	1.6
12688FP	160	12689FP	160	80	128	1.6
12689FP	160	12688FP	160	80	128	1.6
12809FP	280	31626FP	280	140	224	1.6
12811FP	144	4061FP, 10477FP, 12812FP, 12813FP	423	144	230	1.6
12812FP	78	4061FP, 10477FP, 12811FP, 12813FP	423	78	125	1.6
12813FP	103	4061FP, 10477FP, 12811FP, 12812FP	423	103	165	1.6
12871FP	160	12872FP	160	80	128	1.6
12872FP	160	12871FP	160	80	128	1.6
13046FP	320	13047FP, 31629FP, 31630FP, 31631FP, 31632FP, 31633FP	320	46	73	1.6
13047FP	320	13046FP, 31629FP, 31630FP, 31631FP, 31632FP, 31633FP	320	46	73	1.6
13808FP	80		0	80	128	1.6
13961FP	80	31638FP	80	40	64	1.6
14153FP	40	31603FP	200	40	64	1.6
14488FP	40		0	40	64	1.6
14856FP	100	6419FP, 6420FP, 9175FP, 14857FP, 14861FP, 14862FP, 14863FP	1,254	33	52	1.6
14857FP	260	6419FP, 6420FP, 9175FP, 14856FP, 14861FP, 14862FP, 14863FP	1,254	85	136	1.6
14860FP	160	31643FP	160	65	**152.6**	2.4
14861FP	260	6419FP, 6420FP, 9175FP, 14856FP, 14857FP, 14862FP, 14863FP	1,254	53	**83.8**	1.6
14862FP	390	6419FP, 6420FP, 9175FP, 14856FP, 14857FP, 14861FP, 14863FP	1,254	152	**239.2**	1.6
14863FP	130	6419FP, 6420FP, 9175FP, 14856FP, 14857FP, 14861FP, 14862FP	1,254	133	**209.8**	1.6
15295FP	60		0	60	96	1.6
15550FP	320		0	320	512	1.6

Appendix 5. Permitted acres, commingled acres, estimated irrigated acres, and estimated average annual withdrawals from decreed irrigation wells with final permits in the Lost Creek Designated Ground Water Basin.—Continued

[acre-ft, acre-feet]

Permit number[1]	Number of permitted acres[1]	Permit numbers of commingled wells[1]	Number of commingled acres[1]	Estimated number of irrigated acres[2]	Estimated average annual withdrawal[3] (acre-ft)	Estimated average annual application[4] (acre-ft/acre)
15756FP	120	31567FP	40	100	160	1.6
16558FP	40	25278FP	80	27	43	1.6
1730FP	160	1731FP	160	80	**188.2**	2.3
1731FP	160	1730FP	160	77	**181.2**	2.3
1771FP	320	1772FP, 1773FP, 1774FP	320	87	**129.0**	1.5
1772FP	320	1771FP, 1773FP, 1774FP	320	112	**166.2**	1.5
1773FP	320	1771FP, 1772FP, 1774FP	320	76	**112.4**	1.5
1774FP	320	1771FP, 1772FP, 1773FP	320	26	**38.8**	1.5
1775FP	80		0	80	128	1.6
1827FP	80		0	80	128	1.6
19881FP	80		0	80	128	1.6
20140FP	160	6561FP, 31658FP	480	96	154	1.6
2245FP	260	31644FP, 31523FP	260	87	139	1.6
25278FP	80	16558FP	80	53	85	1.6
25FP	80		0	80	128	1.6
26510FP	40		0	40	64	1.6
2665FP	160		0	160	256	1.6
31509FP	80		0	80	128	1.6
31510FP	120	31511FP	120	60	96	1.6
31511FP	120	31511FP	120	60	96	1.6
31512FP	160	72FP	160	80	128	1.6
31513FP	85	31514FP, 78FP	85	28	45	1.6
31514FP	85	31513FP, 78FP	85	28	45	1.6
31515FP	80	31516FP, 31517FP	80	27	43	1.6
31516FP	80	31515FP, 31517FP	80	27	43	1.6
31517FP	80	31515FP, 31516FP	80	27	43	1.6
31518FP	640	31519FP, 31520FP	640	168	**160.8**	1.0
31519FP	640	31518FP, 31520FP	640	144	**137.4**	1.0
31520FP	640	31518FP, 31519FP	640	254	**243**	1.0
31521FP	80		0	80	128	1.6
31522FP	160	31588FP, 31589FP	160	53	85	1.6
31523FP	260	31644FP, 2245FP	260	87	139	1.6
31524FP	160	31525FP	160	80	128	1.6
31525FP	160	31524FP	160	80	128	1.6
31526FP	280	31527FP	280	145	**243.6**	1.7
31527FP	280	31526FP	280	120	**202.2**	1.7
31528FP	320	7244FP	320	160	256	1.6
31529FP	135		0	135	216	1.6
31530FP	80	31540FP, 5866FP, 5867FP	342	29	46	1.6
31531FP	170	31532FP	170	85	136	1.6
31532FP	170	31531FP	170	85	136	1.6
31533FP	372	31534FP, 31535FP	372	124	198	1.6
31534FP	372	31533FP, 31535FP	372	124	198	1.6
31535FP	372	31533FP, 31534FP	372	124	198	1.6
31536FP	80		0	68	**136.0**	2.0
31537FP	240	31538FP	240	120	192	1.6
31538FP	240	31537FP	240	120	192	1.6
31539FP	296	31541FP	296	148	237	1.6
31540FP	182	31530FP, 5866FP, 5867FP	342	65	104	1.6
31541FP	296	31539FP	296	148	237	1.6
31542FP	223		0	205	**307.6**	1.5
31543FP	480	31649FP	480	240	384	1.6
31544FP	80		0	80	128	1.6
31545FP	160		0	160	256	1.6
31546FP	160		0	160	256	1.6

Appendix 5. Permitted acres, commingled acres, estimated irrigated acres, and estimated average annual withdrawals from decreed irrigation wells with final permits in the Lost Creek Designated Ground Water Basin.—Continued

[acre-ft, acre-feet]

Permit number[1]	Number of permitted acres[1]	Permit numbers of commingled wells[1]	Number of commingled acres[1]	Estimated number of irrigated acres[2]	Estimated average annual withdrawal[3] (acre-ft)	Estimated average annual application[4] (acre-ft/acre)
31547FP	160	31548FP	160	80	128	1.6
31548FP	160	31547FP	160	80	128	1.6
31549FP	160	31550FP	160	80	128	1.6
31550FP	160	31549FP	160	80	128	1.6
31551FP	90	31552FP, 31553FP	90	30	48	1.6
31552FP	90	31551FP, 31553FP	90	30	48	1.6
31553FP	90	31551FP, 31552FP	90	30	48	1.6
31554FP	480	31555FP, 31614FP	480	160	256	1.6
31555FP	480	31554FP, 31614FP	480	160	256	1.6
31556FP	360	31557FP	360	180	288	1.6
31557FP	360	31556FP	360	180	288	1.6
31558FP	80		0	80	128	1.6
31559FP	80		0	80	128	1.6
31560FP	204	7602FP	204	102	163	1.6
31561FP	160	31562FP	240	120	192	1.6
31562FP	160	31561FP	240	120	192	1.6
31563FP	134		0	134	214	1.6
31564FP	134		0	134	214	1.6
31565FP	293	10870FP, 10869FP	293	98	156	1.6
31566FP	260	31567FP	180	170	272	1.6
31567FP	220	31566FP, 15756FP	220	110	176	1.6
31568FP	640	9430FP	640	320	512	1.6
31569FP	180	31571FP, 31570FP	180	77	123	1.6
31570FP	60	31569FP, 31571FP	180	26	42	1.6
31571FP	180	31569FP, 31570FP	180	77	123	1.6
31572FP	240	31573FP	240	120	192	1.6
31573FP	240	31572FP	240	120	192	1.6
31574FP	60		0	60	96	1.6
31575FP	160	11708FP, 5035FP	160	53	85	1.6
31576FP	80		0	80	128	1.6
31577FP	160		0	160	256	1.6
31578FP	160		0	160	256	1.6
31580FP	128	10717FP, 31581FP	128	43	68	1.6
31581FP	128	31580FP, 10717FP	128	43	68	1.6
31582FP	200	31583FP	200	100	160	1.6
31583FP	200	31582FP	200	100	160	1.6
31584FP	244	31585FP, 31586FP	244	81	130	1.6
31585FP	244	31584FP, 31586FP	244	81	130	1.6
31586FP	240	31584FP, 31585FP	244	81	130	1.6
31588FP	160	31522FP, 31589FP	160	53	85	1.6
31589FP	160	31522FP, 31588FP	160	53	85	1.6
31590FP	160	31591FP	160	80	128	1.6
31591FP	160	31590FP	160	80	128	1.6
31592FP	160	31593FP	160	80	128	1.6
31593FP	160	31592FP	160	80	128	1.6
31594FP	130		0	130	208	1.6
31595FP	160		0	138	**152.0**	1.1
31596FP	75		0	75	120	1.6
31598FP	65	8821FP	65	33	52	1.6
31599FP	240	31600FP, 31601FP, 31602FP	240	60	96	1.6
31600FP	240	31599FP, 31601FP, 31602FP	240	60	96	1.6
31601FP	240	31599FP, 31600FP, 31602FP	240	60	96	1.6
31602FP	240	31599FP, 31600FP, 31601FP	240	60	96	1.6
31603FP	160	14153FP	200	160	256	1.6
31604FP	160		0	160	256	1.6

Appendix 5.   Permitted acres, commingled acres, estimated irrigated acres, and estimated average annual withdrawals from decreed irrigation wells with final permits in the Lost Creek Designated Ground Water Basin.—Continued

[acre-ft, acre-feet]

Permit number[1]	Number of permitted acres[1]	Permit numbers of commingled wells[1]	Number of commingled acres[1]	Estimated number of irrigated acres[2]	Estimated average annual withdrawal[3] (acre-ft)	Estimated average annual application[4] (acre-ft/acre)
31605FP	160		0	160	256	1.6
31606FP	160		0	160	256	1.6
31607FP	160	31608FP, 31609FP	480	160	256	1.6
31608FP	160	31607FP, 31609FP	480	160	256	1.6
31609FP	160	31607FP, 31608FP	480	160	256	1.6
31610FP	173	31611FP	304	172	275	1.6
31611FP	132	31610FP	304	132	211	1.6
31612FP	117		0	112	**102.8**	0.9
31613FP	160		0	160	256	1.6
31614FP	480	31554FP, 31555FP	480	160	256	1.6
31615FP	160		0	160	256	1.6
31617FP	280		0	280	448	1.6
31618FP	280		0	280	448	1.6
31619FP	480	4263FP, 31620FP, 31621FP, 31622FP	480	96	154	1.6
31620FP	480	4263FP, 31619FP, 31621FP, 31622FP	480	96	154	1.6
31621FP	480	4263FP, 31619FP, 31620FP, 31622FP	480	96	154	1.6
31622FP	480	4263FP, 31619FP, 31620FP, 31621FP	480	96	154	1.6
31623FP	160		0	160	256	1.6
31624FP	160	7788FP	160	80	128	1.6
31625FP	160	31627FP	160	80	128	1.6
31626FP	280	12809FP	280	140	224	1.6
31627FP	160	31625FP	160	80	128	1.6
31629FP	320	13046FP, 13047FP, 31630FP, 31631FP, 31632FP, 31633FP	320	46	73	1.6
31630FP	320	13046FP, 13047FP, 31629FP, 31631FP, 31632FP, 31633FP	320	46	73	1.6
31631FP	320	13046FP, 13047FP, 31629FP, 31630FP, 31632FP, 31633FP	320	46	73	1.6
31632FP	320	13046FP, 13047FP, 31629FP, 31630FP, 31631FP, 31633FP	320	46	73	1.6
31633FP	320	13046FP, 13047FP, 31629FP, 31630FP, 31631FP, 31632FP	320	46	73	1.6
31634FP	173		0	173	277	1.6
31635FP	363		0	363	581	1.6
31636FP	191	31637FP	191	96	153	1.6
31637FP	191	31636FP	191	96	153	1.6
31638FP	80	13961FP	80	40	64	1.6
31639FP	147		0	147	235	1.6
31640FP	157		0	157	**353.0**	2.2
31641FP	160		0	160	256	1.6
31642FP	85	31667FP	85	35	56	1.6
31643FP	160	14860FP	160	82	**194.4**	2.4
31644FP	260	31523FP, 2245FP	260	87	139	1.6
31645FP	160		0	160	256	1.6
31646FP	160	31647FP	160	80	128	1.6
31647FP	160	31646FP	160	80	128	1.6
31648FP	80		0	80	128	1.6
31649FP	480	31543FP	480	240	384	1.6
31650FP	228	31651FP, 9018FP	228	76	122	1.6
31651FP	228	31650FP, 9018FP	228	76	122	1.6

Appendix 5. Permitted acres, commingled acres, estimated irrigated acres, and estimated average annual withdrawals from decreed irrigation wells with final permits in the Lost Creek Designated Ground Water Basin.—Continued

[acre-ft, acre-feet]

Permit number[1]	Number of permitted acres[1]	Permit numbers of commingled wells[1]	Number of commingled acres[1]	Estimated number of irrigated acres[2]	Estimated average annual withdrawal[3] (acre-ft)	Estimated average annual application[4] (acre-ft/acre)
31652FP				92	172.8	1.9
31653FP	320	31652FP, 31654FP	320	67	126.8	1.9
31654FP	320	31652FP, 31653FP	320	87	162.8	1.9
31656FP	120	31657FP	120	60	96	1.6
31657FP	120	31656FP	120	60	96	1.6
31658FP	320	20140FP, 6561FP	480	192	307	1.6
31659FP	80		0	80	128	1.6
31667FP	120	31642FP	85	50	80	1.6
368FP	158	369FP, 370FP	158	53	84	1.6
369FP	158	368FP, 370FP	158	53	84	1.6
370FP	158	368FP, 369FP	158	53	84	1.6
4061FP	58	10477FP, 12811FP, 12812FP	423	58	93	1.6
4263FP	480	31619FP, 31620FP, 31621FP, 31622FP	480	96	154	1.6
4497FP	80	11981FP	80	40	64	1.6
464FP	160	467FP	160	36	68.6	1.9
465FP	160	466FP	160	80	128	1.6
466FP	160	465FP	160	80	128	1.6
467FP	160	464FP	160	42	79.2	1.9
5035FP	160	31575FP, 11708FP	160	53	85	1.6
5036FP	80	12470FP	80	40	64	1.6
510FP	320	7245FP	320	160	256	1.6
5369FP	134		0	134	214	1.6
5370FP	134		0	134	214	1.6
5371FP	134		0	134	214	1.6
5866FP	342	31530FP, 31540FP, 5867FP	342	124	198	1.6
5867FP	342	31530FP, 31540FP, 5866FP	342	124	198	1.6
6419FP	900	6420FP, 9175FP, 14856FP, 14857FP, 14861FP, 14862FP, 14863FP	1,254	294	470	1.6
6420FP	900	6419FP, 9175FP, 14856FP, 14857FP, 14861FP, 14862FP, 14863FP	1,254	294	470	1.6
6561FP	320	20140FP, 31658FP	480	192	307	1.6
7105FP	240	9630FP	240	120	192	1.6
7107FP	80		0	80	128	1.6
7108FP	160		0	160	256	1.6
7200FP	80		0	80	128	1.6
7201FP	80	7203FP	80	40	64	1.6
7202FP	160		0	160	256	1.6
7203FP	80	7201FP	80	40	64	1.6
7244FP	320	31528FP	320	160	256	1.6
7245FP	320	510FP	320	160	256	1.6
7277FP	80		0	80	128	1.6
72FP	160	31512FP	160	80	128	1.6
7602FP	204	31560FP	204	102	163	1.6
7788FP	160	31624FP	160	80	128	1.6
78FP	85	31513FP, 31514FP	85	28	45	1.6
8298FP	80		0	80	128	1.6
8499FP	80		0	80	128	1.6
8500FP	62		0	62	99	1.6
8505FP	160	8506FP	160	80	128	1.6
8506FP	160	8505FP	160	80	128	1.6

Appendix 5. Permitted acres, commingled acres, estimated irrigated acres, and estimated average annual withdrawals from decreed irrigation wells with final permits in the Lost Creek Designated Ground Water Basin.—Continued

[acre-ft, acre-feet]

Permit number[1]	Number of permitted acres[1]	Permit numbers of commingled wells[1]	Number of commingled acres[1]	Estimated number of irrigated acres[2]	Estimated average annual withdrawal[3] (acre-ft)	Estimated average annual application[4] (acre-ft/acre)
8508FP	160		0	160	256	1.6
8533FP	320	8534FP, 8535FP	320	85	**111.4**	1.3
8534FP	320	8533FP, 8535FP	320	88	**115.4**	1.3
8535FP	320	8533FP, 8534FP	320	101	**132.4**	1.3
8619FP	81	8620FP	162	81	130	1.6
8620FP	81	8619FP	162	81	130	1.6
8780FP	20		0	20	32	1.6
8821FP	65	31598FP	65	33	52	1.6
8873FP	320	8874FP, 9321FP	320	100	**109.2**	1.1
8874FP	320	8873FP, 9321FP	320	62	**68.4**	1.1
9018FP	228	31651FP, 31650FP	228	76	122	1.6
9174FP	160		0	160	256	1.6
9175FP	900	6419FP, 6420FP, 14856FP, 14857FP, 14861FP, 14862FP, 14863FP	1,254	294	470	1.6
9321FP	80	8873FP, 8874FP	320	71	**78.2**	1.1
9430FP	640	31568FP	640	320	512	1.6
9521FP	115	9522FP	280	115	184	1.6
9522FP	165	9521FP	280	165	264	1.6
9523FP	132		0	132	211	1.6
9594FP	140		0	140	224	1.6
9595FP	140		0	140	224	1.6
9596FP	140		0	140	224	1.6
9597FP	140		0	140	224	1.6
9598FP	140		0	140	224	1.6
9601FP	140		0	140	224	1.6
9630FP	240	7105FP	240	120	192	1.6
Total				27,835	44,266	
Average of irrigation wells with power-use data				103	157.2	1.6
Average of irrigation wells lacking power-use data				105	168	1.6
Average of all wells				105	166	1.6

[1]Data provided by Suzanne Sellers, Colorado Division of Water Resources (written commun., 2006).

[2] Number of acres irrigated by wells with power-use data was estimated by apportioning the average number of planted acres during 1990–94 with respect to the average annual withdrawal from each well during 1990–94. Number of acres irrigated by wells lacking power-use data was estimated by apportioning the total number of commingled acres with respect to the number of acres permitted for each well.

[3] Average annual withdrawals in bold are estimated from power-use records during 1990–94. Data for wells with power-use records provided by William Fronczac, Gateway American Resources (written commun., 2005). Average annual withdrawals from wells lacking power-use data are estimated as the average annual withdrawal per unit area (1.6 acre-ft/acre) of all wells with power-use data, multiplied by the estimated number of irrigated acres.

[4]Average annual application for wells with power-use data are calculated as the average annual withdrawal divided by the estimated number of irrigated acres. Average annual application for wells lacking power-use data is assumed equal to the average application (1.6 acre-ft/acre) by wells with power-use records.

www.ingramcontent.com/pod-product-compliance
Lightning Source LLC
Chambersburg PA
CBHW080428290526
45791CB00008BA/2433